D1562546

Holy Bones, Limbo, and Jesus in My Cheetos

Catholics Believe the Darndest Things!

Danielle Schaaf

To Abby, for without her inquiring Baptist mind, I might never have written this book.

Mea Culpa, Mea Culpa, Mea Culpa

If you're too young or not Catholic enough to have attended a Latin Mass, *mea culpa* means "through my fault." If you have attended a Latin Mass and didn't remember its meaning, beat yourself on the chest three times and repeat after me: "Through my fault, through my fault, through my fault." If it rings a bell, go ahead and replace your last admonition with "my most grievous fault."

You may assume my mea culpa is an apology for this book's brassy title, bold cover design, and cheeky narrative on the pages to follow. True, those adjectives paint an accurate picture (thank you, Sr. Veronica for "ahem" sharing those descriptors with me), but my mea culpa is for not becoming a nun. I must have the "nun stuff" because I've been mistaken for one several times. Attendees at signings and presentations for my book *Don't Chew Jesus!* often asked if I was a sister, or if I ever had been. I must've been shooting sister vibes out the back of my head because there's no way I looked the part. How many nuns have you seen that color their hair, wear makeup, leather jackets, and boots? Sisters of Perpetual Indulgence don't count.

If I had been a nun, I might have been able to answer some of their next questions, such as: *"I don't remember much from Catholic school—did we really practice all those beliefs?"* and *"Do Catholics believe all those weird things?"*

Mea culpa.

Since I'm not a nun, my first inclination was to drop into the local convent and ask a sister. Little problem. Try finding a convent, much less a nun, these days. So, I did the next best thing. Basking in my glowing nun aura, I took a stab at addressing some of the more notable curiosities on my own. *Holy Bones, Limbo, and Jesus in my Cheetos* is a compilation of the answers to these questions and more, such as: *Who runs the Church? How do you become a saint? "Why is there dirt on your forehead?* And my personal favorite: *Catholics aren't Christians, are they?* These important topics are addressed with my tongue implanted in my cheek.

Mea culpa.

A word of warning: my religious training ended in eighth grade, when I graduated from St. Luke Catholic School. I am still a practicing Catholic, up-to-date on my sacraments, and I raised my kids Catholic. My three adult children remain Catholic, and probably do a better job understanding and practicing the beliefs than I. Unlike my kids, I can't say I've attended Mass said by the pope.

Mea culpa.

I no longer have a Sister of Mercy drilling me on my Catholic catechism, so my examples and explanations are theologically thin. Thinner than the paper they're written on. Thinner than a Girl Scout Thin Mint cookie. Thinner than the I-have-a-headache-excuse thin. Nothing in this book is technically incorrect, but let's just say the Church won't award it an Imprimatur, its *Good Housekeeping-ish* seal of approval for Catholic literature.

Mea culpa.

Because this is written from my experiences and not scholarly research (unless you call Google scholarly), much of the perspective dates back to my childhood Catholic-school days. Think of me as your granny, rocking on the porch and regaling you with stories that begin with "In my day…" Just like Granny, some of my recollections may seem outdated. I've tried reconciling those situations, but for the sake of brevity and humor, I might have come up short. Sort of like if your granny tried to hustle from her seat on the porch to the seat in the bathroom, but only made it as far as the living room. You wouldn't yell, "Burn the old bag!" would you? So be it with me.

Mea culpa.

Before you get your rosaries in a wad and petition the pope to reinstate the Inquisitions, know that I wrote this book with the intention to clarify, or at least draw interest to, what makes a Catholic *Catholic.* If the book sparks a walk down memory lane, a lively discussion, or the desire to learn more about Catholicism, it will have achieved its purpose. All the better if it's accompanied by a hearty laugh.

No mea culpa.

As a penitential offering, I've added resources at the end of the book to provide a fuller, more reputable discussion about our Catholic beliefs, practices, and traditions.

About the title. You're probably wondering if we believe in Holy Bones, Limbo, and Jesus in Cheetos. Holy Bones, absolutely. Limbo, not anymore. Jesus in Cheetos? C'mon, read the book and find out for yourself.

Contents

Who Are Those Darned Catholics?

Danielle Schaaf

You Know He's Catholic If ...

Just because you spent a week Netflixing *Sopranos* don't assume you can spot a Catholic in a crowd. Sure, an "I honk for nuns" bumper sticker might be a dead giveaway. Or not. Maybe the driver is a fan of punk rock. And that coworker eating a Filet-O-Fish every Friday? He may be cutting back on red meat consumption. There's more to figuring out who's Catholic than relying on stereotypes. Give it a shot:

A. A pregnant woman corrals eight kids into her fifteen-seat van in the movie theater parking lot. The marquee advertises a Disney movie marathon.

You're probably thinking, *I got this one*. Catholics pop out so many babies, even rabbits are impressed. Plus, they pledge to not watch inappropriate movies.

B. A group of young boys strolling down the street are wearing matching red t-shirts and baggy gym shorts. Rosary beads (don't worry, I'll explain later) hang from their necks.

Easy peasy. You know red is the team color for St. Ann Catholic School around the corner. Those boys must be St. Ann Crusaders on their way to basketball practice.

C. A man plays a round of golf every Sunday morning.

No way this dude is Catholic, or even Christian, you're thinking as you pat yourself on the back. He's hitting the back nine instead of the pew. Catholics don't miss Mass (don't worry, I'll explain later).

Let's take another look. The woman with the passel of kids may or may not be Catholic. True, Catholic practices eschew birth control but do endorse natural family planning—a scientific, moral, and natural way to achieve or postpone pregnancy. Gone are the days when we relied on "the rhythm method," which had the reliability of your satellite TV in a downpour. These days, that lady hustling her kids could just as easily be Michelle Duggar. Or a Mormon. Both out-birth Catholics three-to-one.

You've got part of your assumptions right about the boys. Knock a couple of days off your stay in Purgatory (I'll explain later, but you might want to start worrying) by recognizing the Catholic rosaries. However, we store our beads in pouches and tuck them away in pockets or purses when not praying with them. Good Catholic schoolchildren would never treat their rosaries like cheap bling. And the matching shirt colors? If they're not wearing tan, black, or plaid, those boys are more likely Crips than Crusaders.

As for the golfer, just because he's teeing off on the 18th hole about the same time you're passing the plate in church, you can't assume he's not Catholic. Give yourself a bonus point if you're thinking: *Hey, aren't Catholics required to attend church every Sunday?* True, missing Sunday Mass can result in a grave sin, a black mark on the soul that could slam our golfer straight to hell. Not even if he's playing with Jack Nicklaus, who's spotted him thirty strokes, would a round of golf be worth spending eternity in a fire pit.

Like the IRS, the Catholic Church offers a loophole. Most churches schedule three or four Masses on Sunday morning, as well as one on Saturday and Sunday evenings. With a schedule like that, the guy can get in thirty-six holes plus a couple of rounds at the bar and still make it to Mass.

Don't flog yourself over your quiz results. Pray three Our Fathers and rent *The Bells of St. Mary*.

Just Who Are Catholics?

The Catholic Church is a community made up of members here on earth, and those in heaven. Despite claims suggesting otherwise, Catholics are Christian. In fact, we get all braggy and like to say, "We're the original followers of Jesus Christ. Catholicism started when Jesus appointed Peter our leader and first pope." Boy, that riles some folks but then we puff up and drive home that point. Beginning with our current pope, we can trace back 2,000 years of Church history pope by pope. Pope Francis I, Pope Benedict XVI, Pope John Paul II…Pope Cletus, Pope Linus, Pope Peter. I toss out this nugget when stuck trying to explain how we Catholics can be Christians, when most of us recite scripture like Donald Trump spouting "two Corinthians" at a campaign rally.

Being Catholic is like having a membership in an extremely large and nonexclusive club. We're governed by rules and led by a hierarchy of leaders. We're awarded plenty of perks, the least of which is the chance to spend eternity in heaven with God. Membership is international and includes more than one billion people. Nearly one out of every four Americans is Catholic.

Although in places like Boston or Chicago you can't step inside a bar without bumping into a fellow Catholic, we're not highly visible in all communities. In some remote areas cut off from basic necessities, like indoor plumbing or four bars of cellphone service, you can drive for miles without passing another Catholic. Hike the Himalayan Mountains or drive through Eastern Tennessee and see for yourself.

Still, we number many and yet our Catholic beliefs, traditions, and practices remain a mystery to most—including to many of us Catholics.

Heavenly Catholics

Just like Chicago ballot-stuffers, Catholics include among our rolls a bajillion people who are dead. Unlike ballot-stuffers, who couldn't care less where those souls reside, we only count Catholics in heaven and not hell (even if they were Catholics when alive).

Leading the Catholic fold in heaven are the Holy Trinity: God the Father, God the Son (Jesus) and God the Holy Spirit. Then there's Mary, the Mother of God/Jesus, angels, and saints.

Most other Christians are pretty much on the same page with their beliefs about God, Jesus, and the Holy Spirit, but where we differ are with Mary, saints, and angels. In fact, there are even wild misconceptions! I'll try to clear up some of those.

Mary

Hand-chosen by God the Father to be Jesus's mother, Mary was an obedient and loving servant. Born without the stain of Adam and Eve's sin, she was as perfect as they come, and she doted on her son. Think of her as a Jewish-Italian-Irish-Greek mom all rolled into one. Because she is Jesus's mother, and Jesus is God, we consider Mary the Mother of God. This doesn't mean we place Mary higher than God or that we worship her. We do ask for her intercession when things get rough. Think about it. When you need help convincing your boss you need a raise, don't you ask those closest to him to put in a good word?

As a good Jewish boy, albeit divine and sinless, Jesus revered His mother. If it's good enough for Jesus, it's good enough for the rest of us Catholics. Anyone who's got problems with that, I'll say a Hail Mary on their behalf.

Saints: Holy Go-to Guys

Saints are men and women who started here on earth, humans like you and me. They died, went to heaven, and are officially recognized as holier-than-thou. Makes sense. Saints suffered intensely, lived virtuously (most of the time), and whipped out miracles on par with a Stephen Spielberg production.

Moral ports in our personal storms, saints serve as patrons invoking our pleas to pray on our behalf. We've got a go-to saint for every cause imaginable, as well as unimaginable. Doc shows you X-rays of your liver and it's shriveled from cancer. You turn to St. Peregrine. In the battle against moles, Saint Ulric is your guy. Those would be the furry beasts tearing up your lawn, not the splotches tearing up your face. The splotches fall under St. Bartholomew's territory, Patron Saint of Dermatology. Some saints carry a heavier load than others, like St. Julian the Hospitaller. He's Patron Saint of Hotelkeepers, Fiddlers, Carnival Workers, and Murderers.

Saints score their own holidays, or feast days, that we dedicate to praying and partying in their honor. Saints' feast days are like Presidents' Day or Cinco de Mayo, minus the sales and salsa.

Once a Saint, Always a Saint. Or Not.

Before you glom onto your next-best-saint-friend, a word of caution: sainthood is not a guaranteed everlasting gig. How crappy it must be to make it all the way to sainthood—maybe after a flogging or a few dozen arrows slung through your chest—only to get demoted to the B-List for no other reason than Church muckety-mucks decide you might not have existed.

Case in point is poor St. Christopher, celebrated centuries for carrying the Christ-child across a raging river. He is still considered a saint by many and has his own feast day, but he's not officially recognized on the Church's roster, the Canon of Saints. The Church says he existed and most likely died a martyr, but his toting Jesus across the river is merely a legend.

I get it. That kid-carrying might have been a stretch, considering Jesus held the record for "walking on water." You've got to admit, aquatic feats aside, there's plenty of proof Christopher had the saintly stuff. Think of all those car crashes that never took place because drivers placed plastic St. Christopher statues on their dashboards. Bobble-headed hula dancers can't lay claim to that. Even though St. Christopher's protective record might have been good enough to earn the Ralph Nader Safe at Any Speed Award, it wasn't enough for official recognition.

Had social media been around, St. Christopher might have fared better. He'd be halfway across the river and a photo of him with Jesus hoisted on his shoulder would've been posted on Instagram #miraclesdohappen. After receiving a few hundred "likes," a movement would begin and then someone would tweet #ChristopherforSaint. Thousands would retweet and the photo would land on Facebook. After 10,000 "likes" and thousands of "shares," the photo would go Chewbacca-laughing-mom viral. The Vatican would then examine the evidence, cross-check at Snopes.com, and then declare St. Christopher's toting of the Christ child the real deal. *Inside Edition* would pick it up and it would be on the cover of *People*. Boom! Saint Christopher would remain on the calendar and Chinese factory workers would shoot fireworks celebrating increased orders for his saintly swag.

Let it Be: Sainthood's Long and Winding Road

Saints aren't chosen because the pope hops out of bed and says, "Hey, I'm gonna name a saint. Saint Lucy the Chaste has a nice ring to it." Reaching sainthood means a candidate has navigated a multilayered process, where he's met a certain set of criteria before advancing to the next level of examination.

It's like playing a video game, only live-action. You've got your warrior knight who's trying to head to the Great Hall and join the King's feast. The knight doesn't walk in and plop down at the table. He must prove himself worthy. First, you find him at the lowest level, in the dungeon. He's got to slay his guard to get out. After stepping over the dead sentinel, your knight moves to another challenge, like swimming in a crocodile-infested moat. After surviving a series of deadly encounters, and moving up in levels of accomplishment each time, your knight reaches the kingdom. That is, until your wife says she's leaving unless you shut off the damn game.

Before candidates for sainthood reach the highest level, Canonization, they go through specific steps, or declarations. First, they are declared Servant of God, followed by Venerable, and then Blessed. Some don't make it through all the stages but no matter where they land, they're still pretty damned holy.

The sainting process is lengthy. Candidates undergo intense scrutiny, on par with a Senate confirmation hearing. Makes sense. There's a lot at stake, like licensing saints' images, book deals, movie rights, and squeezing in another feast day on an already overcrowded calendar. Specific criteria must be met, including living a holy life and having performed two miracles.

Miracles range from run-of-the-mill healings to outside-the-box levitations and bilocations (being in two places at once). Some occur years after a saint's death. One common post-mortem miracle is incorruptibility of the deceased's body. That's when long after his/her death, a saint-to-be's body is exhumed from the grave and found free of decay. Naturally, this is a miracle. Even a lifetime of brushing with Crest can't keep away that kind of decay.

Saint Catherine of Siena is one example of a saint accorded the miracle of incorruptibility. She died in the fourteenth century and 600 years later her body was dug up, completely intact with no decomposition. Her burial was in the days before embalming, back when bodies turned to pulpy mush, resembling ground beef left in the backseat of a car for a week. (Not that I personally know what ground beef looks like after a week in the backseat of a car. Two days, maybe, three tops, but an entire week? That's just plain irresponsible.)

It boggles my mind how exactly the Church got into the grave-digging business. Maybe one night after a raucous jousting match, where more than a few pints of ale-quaffing went down, the pope and his cardinal buddies decided a road trip to the local cemetery was in order. Boys will be boys, you know.

Word on the street is the Church is moving away from relying on incorruptibility as deific evidence for sainthood. With the ever-growing number of cosmetic surgeries, the Vatican's saint gatekeepers are having a tough time determining whether a perfectly dimpled chin is proof of divine intervention or an implant. Plus, they're afraid they'll have to canonize St. Joan Rivers. At least we'd then have a patron saint of plastic surgeons, lifts and tucks, and aging celebrities.

Miracles may be required criteria for sainthood, but dying a painful death is not. Even so, it can't hurt if you die in agony. Take St. Damian of Molokai. A nineteenth century priest, he chose to live among a colony of lepers on a far-off Hawaiian island. Be assured, his stay was no tropical vacation. Leprosy was a slow-moving disease that caused respiratory failure, nerve damage that lead to blindness, and loss of extremities because victims couldn't feel pain. There was no cure. Death was agonizing.

Saint Damian volunteered to live among the infected when no one else dared to go near them. He lived side-by-side with lepers, fearlessly laying his prayerful hands on their heads and placing communion on their tongues. As the colonists lay dying in his arms, he selflessly administered last rite oils and blessings. With that level of exposure, Fr. Damian was bound to suffer the same fate. That day arrived during Molokai Madness Marathon. He and his teammate in the three-legged race crossed the finish line, eking a win by the skin of their noses. Father Damian, ablaze in a Cubs-World-Series-championship victory glow, kissed, back-slapped, and fist-bumped his way into leprosy land. Once there, his skin blistered and sores the size of pepperonis covered his body head-to-toe. That is, until his toes fell off. Eventually, he died from the disease.

Saint Damian certainly died an excruciating death, his suffering earning him sainthood brownie points. Not as many as St. Bartholomew, one of the original apostles. Torturers skinned Saint Bart alive. To think, we go ballistic over waterboarding.

Traffic Jams on the Road to Sainthood

Although unusual, the sainthood process can be fast-tracked for some candidates, as it was for Pope John Paul II. He died in 2005, and was canonized a saint in 2014. That's a nanosecond in saint approval time. Decades typically pass between a person's death and sainthood. That's almost as long as between diagnosis and treatment in a VA hospital.

In some situations, like Saint Joan of Arc's, the process can take hundreds of years. You'd think toasting over an open fire like a boy scout's marshmallow would have put her on sainthood Easy Street. Not quite. Nearly 500 years of research, validation, verification, crossing t's and dotting i's took place before St. Joan was finally canonized. Rumor has it she may have been in for a longer wait if it hadn't been for a five-year-old actress performing in a Vatican variety show in the early twentieth century. In a papal flash of insight, Pope Benedict XV recognized the conversion power little Ingrid Bergman might one day possess by portraying young, brave Joan burning at the stake. Saint Joan was soon granted sainthood and the child's career took off, eventually earning her an Oscar nomination.

Granted, the process moves faster today because there's quicker access to documentation and proof, thanks to 24/7 news coverage. One call to a Catholic producer at CNN, and before Fox News anchor Bill O'Reilly had a chance to offer his fair and balanced opinion, the Vatican's researcher could have gathered almost all the evidence needed to canonize Pope John II. From the pope's skiing and hiking trips, to his visits to more than 100 countries, mounds of news footage lay at the researcher's fingertips.

On the flip side, poor St. Joan's researchers had to rely on a succession of monks-in-the-making holed up in monasteries. Hundreds of years passed as they leafed through Vatican archives, jotting notes with feather quills. No one was sitting at a computer Googling "Joan of Arc" and "fire-proof armor," with a printer nearby spewing out hundreds of documentations. No wonder it took 500 years. It wasn't until then monks gained simple research aids, like electrical lighting and coffee.

The Vatican's Got Saints

Earning the papal Saint Seal of Approval is serious business. The pope doesn't sit in a plush chair with his back to the stage while a Vatican intern sings a saint wannabe's merits. He's not going to whip around and say, "I want her on my team," just because the intern crooned, "Romans threw poor, naked Perpetua into an arena. She battled a wild cow. The cow won." As entertaining as that might be, it's not gonna happen.

Still, interjecting pizzazz into the selection process might create more interest and clear up confusion over how we name saints. Maybe the Church should try a reality TV show. Millions of us tune into *The Biggest Loser* every week. Budweiser and Beer Nuts in hand, we watch trying to guess who the next contestant to get booted off the ranch might be. Will it be the Wichita housewife hoping to lose those extra 100 pounds of baby fat she's been carrying for twenty years? Or how about the Atlanta accountant hoarding Butterfingers candy bars in his sock drawer?

Admit it, reality TV has us sucked in, so why not use a show to demonstrate what it takes to become a saint? Each week, we could tune into VNN and watch the latest installment of *The Vatican's Got Saints*. The Vatican could enlist celebrity judges and televise the process in front of a live audience. Sorta like the Inquisitions but without executions. Here's a glimpse of the pilot:

Nick Cannon, announcing offstage:

"Welcome to *The Vatican's Got Saints!* We're here in the Middle Ages at Wells Cathedral trying to uncover a hidden saint or two. Join us in applause for our renowned judges."

"Mel B!"

"Awe, peace be with you," the former Spice Girl says over and over again, glad-handing with audience members as she heads to her chair at the judge's table.

"Simon Cowell!"

Simon ambles to the front, shaking hands and answering, "Uh, oh, yeah, and, also with you...um, I mean, and with your spirit," to the show's guests offering him the sign of peace.

"Howie Mandel!"

Howie fist-bumps his way to his seat, leaving in his wake a string of mutterings like, "Strange sign of peace," "Maybe it's a Jewish thing," and "Father O'Leary would've kicked his ass after Mass."

The first contestant stands on a spot, center stage. Mel says, "Tell us your name and where you're from."

"Joseph. I flew in from Cupertino ten minutes ago."

"Airplanes haven't been invented yet," Mel says, wrinkling her brow in bewilderment.

"I know."

"Joseph, what miracle will you perform today?" Howie asks.

"Levitation. I'll slip into a trance and then drift to the rafters," the saint-hopeful says. "No pulley, no cables, no hidden tricks. Before I start to rise, I'd like to warm up singing a Gregorian Chant Brother Gregg sang for us in the Allman Monastery.

"'Ramblin' Man' so moved my Allman Brothers."

"We hope it does the same for you, Joseph," Mel says. "Go Ahead."

Joseph closes his eyes. After several minutes rocking back and forth, he hums. Just when patrons begin leaving the auditorium, Joseph belts out a Woodstock-styled rock song. A buzz fills the room. Hands wave in the air, and heads bob back and forth. Bodies sway when Joseph serenades how hard it is to earn a living. The judges rock in their seats, nodding in rhythm.

Joseph's chant hits a crescendo and he belts out a warning that it's time for him to leave. His body lifts off the stage and floats toward the ceiling. Audience members cannot believe the spectacle they're witnessing:

"He's doing it!"

"Where are the wires?"

"Will he crash?"

Engulfed in a flash of light, Joseph zips over the judges' heads. He hovers low enough to part Howie's hair, like Moses and the Red Sea. That is, if Howie had hair.

"Make it so, Number One," Joseph cries out. "Within seconds, he's cruising the vast room, corner-to-corner in warp speed. Before Howie has a chance to say, "Deal or no deal?" Joseph lands on the stage. He faces the judges, a halo circling his head.

"Not bad for a first miracle," Simon says. "What else you got?"

I'm certain ratings would be off the charts for *The Vatican's Got Saints!* but I don't think the Church is ready to walk down that reality TV road. They're not willing to be sandwiched in a timeslot between *RuPaul's Drag Race* and *Hoarders*.

America's Saint Comes Marching In

We may be stuck with the Vatican same ol' same ol' way of selecting saints another millennium, but we don't have to be in the dark about how they are chosen. Let's walk through the process step by step, using America's most likely next saint: Peyton Manning. Makes sense, since he's already a football god.

I realize Manning has a skeleton in his closet. Hanging over his head are nasty allegations Manning sexually harassed a female trainer at the University of Tennessee, where he played football. No sweat. Lesser have made it to sainthood. Our saint rolls are filled with holy men and women who started down the saint trail lugging baggage loaded with scandal, sleaze, and even crime. Hey, if St. Vladimir can make it, so can Manning. When murder, rape, and human sacrifice don't stop a guy from becoming a saint, what's a youthful indiscretion going to do?

Overall, Manning seems to have the saintly stuff. Crowds revere him and consider the ground under his feet hallowed. Folks have glorified his soul ever since his Tennessee Vols days. Besides, it's time we include another American in the holy hood. Only a dozen or so out of 10,000 saints are from the United States.

Step One—Servant of God Declaration

The candidate must first be deemed worthy of sainthood. The Church relies on fact-gathering and input from local clergy who have investigated the candidate's background. They require validation the candidate lived piously, served others, and was considered an all-around swell guy. So far, so good for Manning.

Manning's got a load of evidence in his favor. First, he's the son of a saint. His father, Archie, played for the New Orleans Saints. Second, Manning is a paragon of piety. It doesn't get much more pious than having a children's hospital named after you. As a bonus, Peyton Manning Children's Hospital belongs to a Catholic medical center named after a saint! In the celebrity piety pecking order, he's not quite Oprah, but Brad and Angelina can't touch him. For starters, not only is he still married, Manning isn't marked with the taint of ten years living in sin before taking his marriage vows. It's hard to top that, but it gets better. Word's out he's looking at opening a string of Papa John's in third-world countries and will deliver free pizza to orphanages. Boom, take that Brangelina.

Manning scores high in likability and service. Fan adoration ranks him among the most well-liked in football and so do advertisers. His product endorsements rake in big bucks. No other sports figure this century can touch Manning's saint appeal. Although, one did come close. Experts say he was on track for beatification but was beaten out of his chance by his wife. Literally. With a golf club. His own. Vatican lips aren't sinking ships but sources have confirmed "St. Tiger" would not be added to the saint roster in the foreseeable future.

In a breeze, Manning passes muster. He is beatified and moves closer to sainthood. At this stage, the candidate is designated "Servant of God." However, there's talk Manning will be called "Servant of Staubach."

Step Two—Venerable Declaration

If the Vatican can determine Manning has lived a heroic, virtuous life, he clears the second hurdle. He is venerated. That's the official declaration he's to be revered and from then on called "Venerable Peyton."

Until his last few football seasons, Manning demonstrated little evidence of heroism and virtuosity. Sure, performing on the field under the pressure of living up to superstar Dad Archie, with younger brother Eli nipping at his passing-record ankles, shows valor. That's not exactly a measure of saint aptitude. The Church looks for martyrdom, blood, and guts. We want our saints having undergone excruciating indignities, like having eyes gouged out, breasts lopped off, or spending a lifetime kneeling on hard church floors instead of padded kneelers. Pain and suffering goes a long way in our Catholic world. Just listen to the wails from teenage school girls forced to wear knee-length, plaid skirts instead of neon booty shorts.

Don't get me wrong, Manning's career was not without pain. After all, in schoolyard bouts of Rock-Paper-Scissors determining which Manning is the better quarterback, he loses to Eli every time. Not only ouch, but double ouch. No one really believes Eli is better. As agonizing as ending up with the short stick in a sibling rivalry battle must be, it's not the same as stoned-to-death torture. Except if you're St. Zenobios.

A third-century bishop, St. Zenobios, was arrested in a persecution roundup. He was hung from a trestle as his body was dismembered—while he was alive and kicking. Well, maybe alive and squirming. But, there he was, minding his own pain-laced business when along comes his twin sister, Zenobia. That gal was gunning to out-suffer Zenobios. Not letting her brother get a jump on her fifteen minutes of fame, Zenobia charged his captors and demanded they toss her a torture nugget. Not to refuse an angry Greek woman, persecutors complied. No torture nugget for Zenobia. They threw her a boulder.

First, captors forced Zenobia to lie on an iron bed covered in burning coals. You won't find one of those at Sears. Then, for good measure, they lowered her into a vat of boiling tar. Boy, was Zenobios pissed at Zenobia for stealing his agony points. Granted, he already earned more than his fair share, just by wandering around his village.

"Little Zenobia, fetch me water from the cistern."

"I'm Zenobios. Zenobia is my sister."

"Zenobia, Zenobios. Whatever. Just bring the water. And stop with the matching tunics."

Bottom line, the Vatican needed more agony, more saint-level suffering from Manning. They got their wish his final football season. After incurring a debilitating physical condition, Manning was forced to sit out an entire season. The following year, the Indianapolis Colts cut him. Having a children's hospital bear his name wasn't enough to secure a fifteenth season with the Colts. The final blow, and proof of unbearable anguish, came when *Dancing with the Stars* chose Doug Flutie instead of him.

Any lingering doubts that Manning didn't meet up to saintly standards were put to rest during a press conference after winning his last game, Super Bowl 50. An interviewer asked Manning how he would celebrate. Manning said he'd relax and drink a Bud. On national television, during one of the most-watched shows of the year, Manning plugged a product without being paid. Not once, but twice. Manning generated more than three million dollars in exposure for the beer company and he didn't earn a dime. Gouging his eyes would have hurt less.

At this point, the Vatican venerates Manning and moves to the next step. The Church claims he is now officially revered by all. It's not clear how that went over when Manning told his wife, but I wouldn't be surprised if she's not in the "everyone reveres Peyton" camp. Let that genie out of the bottle and the next thing you know, he'll be telling her he's too revered to carry out the trash.

Step Three—Blessed Declaration

Manning now needs to provide proof of a miracle. Once successful, he climbs up another rung on the sainthood ladder. All will then call him "Blessed Peyton."

We've got a no-brainer. Convincing Head Coach Kubiak that Manning still had what it took in 2014 to quarterback the Broncos to the Super Bowl was, in itself, a miracle. Manning had the worst performance of his career the previous season. All was not wasted that year, though. He chalked up major pain-and-suffering points, earning him the nickname "Manning the Martyr."

The Vatican signs off on his first miracle and he is beatified. One more stop before Blessed Peyton can be called a saint.

Step Four—Saint Declaration

Not relying on one miracle, especially one as thin as his first, the Vatican requires Blessed Peyton chalk up another. If the evidence is convincing, the pope will canonize him St. Peyton Manning.

At age forty, Manning was the oldest starting Super Bowl quarterback in history. That's so old in quarterback years, he should have been renamed Methuselah Manning. Not only did he play in the game, but he also led the team to a resounding win. And all of this with a noodle of a throwing arm! He couldn't pass the ball more than fifteen yards. Surely the Vatican would deem his feat a miracle, one of biblical proportions. Manning winning the Super Bowl at his age was akin to Abraham fathering a child at the age of one hundred.

Even though Manning is now positioned for canonization, he faces a couple of hitches. First, he's not Catholic. That's not a deal breaker. He could convert and join a long list of saints before him. Saint Edith Stein, who was put to death by Nazis in World War II, was born into a Jewish family. She was raised in that faith but eventually turned Catholic. She even became a nun and lived in a convent. The first American-born saint, St. Elizabeth Seton, converted from Episcopalian. She, too, became a nun and lived in a convent. Manning could easily switch to Catholicism, thus becoming eligible for sainthood. No need for him to go all Caitlin Jenner, becoming a nun and living in a convent. The Church would give him a pass on that one.

His biggest obstacle is he's alive. Oh, sure, Manning played lifeless his last few seasons but that's not enough for sainthood. He needs to be dead. As in, a doorknob. Six feet under. Pushing daisies. Pick your tired cliché, they all mean nothing can happened until after his casket is lowered into the ground. From the looks of him, that's a long, long, long way off.

After death, he faces a five-year waiting period before the canonization process is initiated. The time will pass quickly. A year takes on new meaning when you've reached eternal-living status.

Holy Bones, Limbo, and Jesus in My Cheetos

One moment, you're the last guy standing in line at the pearly gates, a few hundred people behind Abraham Lincoln, and the next moment you turn around and see your eighty-year-old grandson behind you.

The wait is worth it. Great things are in store for St. Peyton. He'll get his own feast day, a medal, and a specific cause in which the faithful will ask for his prayers. Bronco fans are rooting for the Patron Saint of Lost Causes, but that's a lost cause. Saint Jude has had a lock on that title for centuries. Saint Peyton might be better suited as Patron Saint of Second Chances.

Angels

Angels are the least mysterious of all heavenly beings. They're everywhere. You can find them on city welcome signs, team logos, and on the back of motorcycle gang members' jackets. Like gang members, they adhere to a hierarchy. Unlike bikers, except for those starring in a 1960s beach movie, angels are a musical bunch. Heaven is home to nine choirs of angels.

Seraphim and Cherubim

Every Catholic school kid from my era recognizes the names of heaven's two top choirs, Seraphim and Cherubim. Nuns had us singing *"Triumph all ye cherubims, sing with us, ye seraphims."* Never mind those lyrics made no sense to most of us. Questioning a nun was not in the picture. Only brown-nosers hanging out with nuns after school realized we were singing about angels.

Except for archangels and angels, the remaining five choirs are unfamiliar to all but angelologists and grandmothers that did time in a convent. Although Choirs of Powers, Virtues, and Dominions continue to live in anonymity, the Choir of Thrones has gained ground in recent years. People get them mixed up with *Game of Thrones*.

Archangels

Considered chief angels, archangels have names and designated responsibilities. Most we've never heard of, but a few stand out. Michael, the leader of the archangels, is well-known. He's recognized for his strength and courage, thanks to battling bad-boy Archangel Lucifer and kicking his butt all the way to hell. Michael is our General Patton in God's army of angels.

Another familiar archangel is Gabriel, a messenger angel oozing charisma and persuasiveness. He makes the Sham Wow guy look like a door-to-door Fuller Brush salesman. His job has been to reveal sensitive decisions from God without setting people off. Gabriel appeared from out of nowhere to an unmarried teenaged girl and told her she was chosen by God to become pregnant and give birth to His son. The son would be holy and rule a kingdom forever. You know the rest of the story. Young Mary agreed. Today, most girls couldn't get beyond the "Behold, I am an angel of the Lord," before spraying him with mace.

Archangel Raphael is also familiar to most of us Catholics, but less for his gift of healing the Old Testament earth and more for his crime-fighting Teenage Mutant Ninja Turtle role.

Guardian Angels

Lowest on the angel totem pole but most widely known, guardians are spiritual bodyguards assigned to each of us on earth. They guide us through dangers and whisper in our ear when we're headed down the wrong path. No one really knows how an angel is assigned his earthly ward. Do they draw straws? Is there a lottery?

Maybe it's as simple as being the next angel in the que. Dozens of God's day laborers hang out on a corner cloud as if it's a Stop-N-Go, waiting for the angel foreman to call out their assignments. Celestials busy themselves playing tiddlywinks or by yakking about which movie was their favorite, *Here Comes Mr. Jordan* or *Heaven Can Wait*. Then, the birth of baby Billy Graham is announced. There's jubilation and back slapping, and off goes the lucky guardian, his halo glowing and a wing-to-wing grin spreading on his cherubic face. Next called out are Desmond Tutu and Timmy Tebow. It's been a good run for the guardians, until the last name of the day:

"Tom Brady."

The next angel in line accepts his assignment. He descends to earth, dragging his harp behind him. He's stuffing cloud bits in his ears to shut out the whispers.

"Tough ride."

"Better luck in eighty years."

"Watch out for deflated balls."

As with all guardian angels, this little guy took his charge to heart. Sure, there were bumps along the way, like being down twenty-five points. The angel kicked into guardian high gear, guiding Brady down the field and into Super Bowl history books with an overtime win.

Fallen Angels

The next time you beat yourself up for screwing up a good thing, like missing out on a Caribbean cruise because nail techs couldn't stop laughing long enough to finish your pedicure before the ship set sail, relax. Others have done worse. Consider Satan, or as he was originally named, Archangel Lucifer.

Not satisfied with serving in the second highest position in heaven for eternity, Lucifer set his sights on the supreme power gig. That's right, he wanted to sit in a throne higher than God's. Even though his name meant shining light, Lucifer must have burnt out more than a few bulbs when he hatched that plan. Not only did he fail to get that throne, God sent his strongman, Archangel Michael, to usher him out of heaven. He got the boot, along with a new name and eternal home.

Falling from heaven into hell, Satan and his followers, called demons, gave birth to the classification "fallen angels." Or, as my mother and other Catholic moms used to call them, "bad angels." "Fallen angels" took on another meaning for our mothers.

Earthly Catholics

Boys in the 'Hood

Someone's gotta run God's show on earth, so, while standing by a huge rock about 2,000 years ago, Jesus put the apostle Peter in charge. A lowly fisherman, he considered taking "Captain Pete" as his new title, but settled upon Pope Peter. That name had rock-star appeal. Plus, it would keep his face off packages of frozen fish sticks down the road. From that moment, the Church put into place a paternal chain of command. Interesting to note, there's a theory that Major League Baseball tried replicating the structure. The MLB came close, with one major exception: the commissioner's position isn't a life-long commitment. Thank goodness.

Pope

The title "pope" comes from the Greek word pappas, which means father. Thus, the pope's authority is supreme and to be carried out in a paternal, fatherly manner. He's like Bud Selig, except he doesn't get booed when he enters stadiums. He's also called other names, including His Holiness and Pontiff, which means "bridge builder." Only in Selig's dreams does anyone call him either of these names.

Cardinal

Next in line after the pope are cardinals, members appointed to assist with governing the Church. They're like baseball team owners, except paid a lot less. Just as with the commissioner, the pope has the final say. Early on in the Church, around the beginning of the sixth century, some members of the papal inner circle suggested they be called blue jays or orioles. The pope shut down discussions, declaring they'd be known as cardinals. Some say the Holy See stepped out on his balcony looking for his pet dove, but instead saw a scarlet bird soaring overhead. A sign from above!

I'm not buying this mystical hooey. In my opinion, his was a fashion-driven decision. The pope wanted to make sure in the annual Vatican Christmas card his white robe popped out against the backdrop of his inner-circle wearing red.

Archbishop

The leader presiding over one or more dioceses, or territories, comprising individual church parishes is known as an archbishop. They're the Church's general managers. Like many baseball general managers who move into that job from their position of team managers, archbishops are promoted up from the ranks of bishop. The promotion doesn't come with a lot of perks, other than first choice of seating at Catholic Ladies Guild charity fashion shows. He wears the same type of clothes as the bishop, lives in the same rectory, and has the same responsibilities with more territory to cover. An archbishop is like one of the handful of employees to survive a corporate layoff and be given a promotion.

Bishop

A bishop oversees parishes and priests within a diocese. He gets to perform special gigs, like ordaining priests, confirming teenagers, and presiding over golf tournaments. He's like MLB managers who are charged with the overall responsibility for running the team.

Priest

Priests are the down-in-the-trenches guys, the intermediaries between parish peons and Church hierarchy. They're our Cal Ripkin Jrs., reporting to work every day and tackling parish duties. Day-in and day-out, priests say Mass, hear confessions, and play Bingo with senior citizens with the gusto of a rookie on his first day in the Majors. Priests are the Church's ironmen.

Brothers

A brother is the generic title originally given to all members of religious communities, but now it generally identifies religious orders of men who have not been ordained priests. A brother shares some similarities with a minor league player waiting for his call up to the

Big Show. Minor league players are important to the team's organization but not very visible, unless you live in a town with a franchise. Brothers are equally as important to the Church's organization, and not as visible, unless one visits your parish. A major difference between brothers and minor league players is brothers aren't waiting to be called up to the priesthood. They're content to stay as brothers, but they balk at being called bros.

Being known as a "brother" has become trendy over the years. It's important to point out these famous brothers are not official Church brothers:

Jonas Brothers

Marx Brothers

Gershwin Brothers

Wright Brothers

Everly Brothers

Baldwin Brothers (Stephen is the only one who stands a chance)

Seminarians

As young men studying for the priesthood, seminarians are like college baseball players. Both groups study, practice, and perform while praying their vocation is the right call for them. Seminarians and baseball players alike are idolized by groupies. One of them has adoring coeds spit-shining their cleats, while the other is surrounded by doting grandmothers polishing their rosary beads.

Monks

Monks are to the Catholic Church what sportswriters are to the MLB. They share similar lifestyles. Monks bunk down in a barren monastery, and sportswriters sleep in roach-infested hotels. Before turning in for the night, monks gather together in a chapel to pray and belt out Latin chants. Sportswriters hang out at the Bylines and Booze Bar, knock down a few belts and chant gibberish before calling it a night.

Let's Hear It for the Girls

They say behind every good man is a woman, and so it is with our Catholic community. However, women hold no official upper echelon positions in the Church's hierarchy. Never mind that God Himself chose a woman to become the mother of His son—a move that saved our asses from eternal damnation—men still call the Catholic shots. Sensing they'd need help in the war on evil, poverty, immorality, and hooliganism in pubescent boys, the Church put forth female foot soldiers: nuns.

An actress in the one-woman-show hit *Late Nite Catechism* quipped nuns were like gangs. They were members in a group, hung out in packs, and dressed alike. I think a more apt comparison would be to sorority girls. Once you factor out makeup, hair straightener, and breast enhancements, that is. Nuns and sorority women both refer to themselves as sisters. They live in communities, dress in matching signature clothing, and share common beliefs. Both types of sisters are big on rituals and proudly wave oversized paddles. Nuns take vows of obedience, poverty, and chastity. Sorority girls vow to watch weekly episodes of *The Bachelor*. Sororities and religious orders of nuns both induct their members through set stages.

Postulant and Pledge (Recruit)

The first step nuns and sorority sisters undertake in their journey to sisterhood is figuring out which group they want to join. Nuns enter as postulants, and their probationary period lasts about six months. Sorority girls start as recruits (formerly known as pledges) and their period—Rush—takes about one week. When a young woman enters the convent, she's greeted with a stern glare and a haircut. Recruits step inside a sorority house and are showered with hugs, air kisses, and selfies.

As soon as recruits enter the house, they face their first ritual: door stacking. Doors are thrown open and the hopefuls face dozens of sisters. Some of the sisters crouch in front with their hands resting on their knees while the other girls stand behind them, all crowding the doorway. Then, they bounce. Up and down, down and up, dozens of girls bob and chant a welcoming ditty. With the orchestrated precision of synchronized swimmers or June Taylor Dancers (Google alert: "June Taylor Dancers"), sorority girls whip their heads left and right, flipping their hair side-to-side like metronomes.

Door stacking dates back decades. Probably after a Panhellenic girls' night out watching *Beach Blanket Bingo*, Zetas, Deltas, and Kappas came together to choreograph a memorable welcome for future sisters. They reasoned door stacking would convince recruits that the house was filled with bubbly, bouncy, and *mostly* blonde versions of Annette Funicello (Google alert: "Annette Funicello"). At this point, brunettes and redheads ducked out for a Clairol run and only hoped no one would wonder "Does she, or doesn't she?" when they sneaked back in.

Girls with short hair faced a fork in the road. Some saw the writing on the recruitment wall and dropped out. Topping their pixie cuts with chi-chi berets, those girls swapped sorority houses for coffee houses. Others, most likely former high school cheerleaders who'd been down that hairy highway before, knew a thing or two about hair adaptations. With confidence, they entered the house, making sure to twirl their high ponytail hairpieces when they introduced themselves.

Postulants and recruits are not the only ones trying to figure out which convent or house is right for them. Leadership in both organizations do the same. It's crucial to figure out if the gals have what it takes to be Mercy or Zeta girls. Until hours late into the night, they toss out questions, "Will she fit in?" "Will she carry on our traditions?" "Will she nurse our hangovers?"

Novice and Prospective New Member (PNP)

A woman enters a religious order as a novice. That's nun-speak for newbie. She receives her order's "habit of clothing," which includes a veil and sensible shoes. She joins other novices in prayer, chores, and mending priests' socks. A novice is generally assigned undesirable tasks, like taking out the trash or washing out Mother Superior's undies. This period lasts about a year. Last Novices kneeling are invited to remain in the convent. Those deemed not-up-to-sisterly-snuff are shown the door and given directions to the nearest Order of the Eastern Star.

Sororities invite prospective new members, PNPs, to join their ranks. Previously, they were invited to "pledge" the sorority as "pledges." Duh. That stopped after a YouTube video "Puking Pretty Pledges of the SEC" went viral. Like novices, PNPs must also serve a probationary period where they learn sorority rules, history, and songs. During that time, they serve their sisters. Among their responsibilities are carrying out grunt duties like being designated driver to tailgating parties or holding back the sorority president's hair while she kneels over the toilet.

Sister and Sister

To become full-fledged sisters in either an order or sorority, women undergo traditional and secret ritual-driven initiations. Both groups require initiates to dress in clothing similar to their sisters before them. This usually entails hitting up Ye Olde Amish Boutique instead of Forever 21.

In a final ceremony, women accept and vow to honor legacies of their orders and sororities. They receive a blessing and are welcomed into a lifelong sisterhood. Sorority girls go on to attend date nights with frat boys. Religious sisters get to escort middle-school boys on field trips to the seminary.

Church Grunts

Rounding out our Catholic community are scrubs, peons, and minions—otherwise known as "The Faithful." We're everyday members holding down the pews from Baltimore to Burma. We are the non-ordained "lay people," parents, children, and ministry volunteers. We are parishioners, the worker bees that keep the Church hive humming.

Cradle Catholics and Converts

The Church has grown tremendously the past forty years but not because we cradle Catholics (those of us born into Catholic families) are churning out kids numbering in the double digits like our parents and grandparents. Much of the expansion has come from members that have converted from other religions. Even though converts rank right behind Polish grannies in their love of the Church, some of their old habits must be difficult to break. As a cradle Catholic who spent her formative years under the influence of nuns, I can pick out a convert in a pew quicker than a prison gang leader can spot a snitch in a cellblock. Here are clues:

1. Converts arrive moments before Mass's opening procession, or even afterward. We cradlers had it drilled into us to arrive fifteen minutes before Mass begins. We were taught to use that time in prayerful preparation for Mass. I call this Catholic mind yoga, without the mats.

2. They don't always bless themselves with holy water when entering or leaving the church. If they're wearing silk blouses or ties, they typically skip the holy watering hole. Not us cradlers. Fugget about a one-finger dip, we plunge in up to our elbows. We've got to make sure we get a thorough hand sloshing, especially on the way out of church. That way, when Father shakes our sopping wet hand, he'll know we're good Catholics.

3. Converts genuflect (kneeling on one knee in a sign of honoring Jesus's presence in the church when entering the pew) on their left knees instead of the requisite right. Even more telling is some converts might not bend all the way down so their knee touches the floor. Another telltale sign of a convert is if they're old enough to collect social security and they've never had knee replacement surgery.

4. They chew Jesus on the way back to pews after receiving communion. Actually, this is becoming a less foolproof ID method, because the last wave of suck-don't-chew-Jesus Catholics are baby boomers. Since the Church reforms in the '60s, we have been allowed to take communion in our hands instead of having the priest place it directly on our tongues. These days, Gen Xer and Millennial cradle Catholics are both as likely as converts to chew.

5. Converts attend, or send their children, to Sunday School. Although Catholic religious education has been administered under a variety of acronyms like CCD and CCE, along with formal titles like "Religious Formation," we cradlers never use the term "Sunday School." Most of our religious education has taken place on days other than Sunday. That's so parishioners don't skip Mass just because we've attended class.

6. Converts refer to Mass as a service or services. For example, "I just got home from Sunday services," or Uncle Max would have liked his funeral service." Uncle Max would probably not be too keen on his funeral Mass being described the same way you would an old-time gas station fill-up.

7. Ditto a priest's sermons. We listen to homilies. The only time Father delivers a sermon is if you confess missing Mass because you scored free box seats to a Texans football game and didn't invite him.

Catholics Believe the Darndest Things

Catholicism 101

Bible

Like Baptism, adhering to Bible teachings is a belief we share with other Christians. Here again, we push Protestant buttons. Our Catholic Bible includes seven more Old Testament books than most denominations' versions.

I've been asked "Why?" many times and have typically answered, "I didn't even know that we had more books." I then follow with, "Are those the books in the front or back of the Bible?" Wipe those holy smirks off your faces. I grew up in a time when we didn't crack open our Bibles in school. No worries. Our nuns made sure we knew what was inside. Except for the Book of Revelations. Sisters relied on other methods to scare the hell out of us.

However, one of the best answers I've ever heard came from a Good Catholic Boy when a classmate proposed the question:

Classmate: "Why does our Bible have seven more books?"

Good Catholic Boy: "King James, sitting on his throne and thinking he'd rather hang out with his knights than spend hours reading his Bible each day, stood up and declared, 'Fee-Fi-Fo-Fum, I'm King of the land.' He then took matters into his own hands. Literally. The King started ripping books out of the Bible. The first was Baruch, next came Judith, and he finally stopped when he tore out Wisdom. By the time he finished, seven Old Testament books lay on the ground. He cut out more than two hours of Bible time! Struck by how the Kingdom's GNP would skyrocket if his peasants had that much more time to till his land, the King ordered the Bible be permanently revised. Hence, the introduction of the King James Bible."

As plausible as this sounds, the boy's answer doesn't exactly jive with Church teachings that are more complex than a pissed-off king pulling out pages. I'm sure the topic made a great conversation piece over the Protestant kid's dinner table, though.

Catechism of the Catholic Church (CCC)

Every time someone asks me, "Do Catholics really believe that crap?" I smile and reach for my copy of *Catechism of the Catholic Church*. The CCC is our Wikipedia, only with impeccable sources. It's our go-to source spelling out our Catholic beliefs and practices. Every. Single. One. With nearly 3,000 entries, it was created in the early 1990s after inquisitive Baby Boomer Catholics thought there had to be more than the nuns' stock response: "It's a divine mystery."

The Ten Commandments

A moral code carried out by most Christians, the Ten Commandments are especially embraced by Catholic mothers. What better guidelines for guilting your kids into doing the right thing than a list of Thou Shalts and Thou Shalt Nots delivered from the mountaintop by the same guy who would one day proclaim, "… *From my cold, dead hands.*" The cheekiest hell raisers from my schooldays thought twice about pilfering even one piece of Bazooka bubble gum from the corner store. If they didn't fear being struck down by Moses in heaven, they worried like hell that Ben Hur would run them over in his Chariot. Or at least that a station wagon filled with nuns would.

One unusual tidbit I never realized until adulthood is we Catholics list a different set of Ten Commandments than do some other Christian denominations. Notably missing, as many Evangelicals like to point out, is the directive about not worshipping graven images. Some accuse early Church leaders of purposely dropping that commandment. Not true. In the words of parents trying to explain why it's okay for them to smoke and drink but it's not okay if their kids do: "It's complicated." The omission results from an editing difference because of how chapters and verses were laid out in

Catholic and Protestant Bibles. Rest assured, there's no truth that medieval woodworkers pressed for the "graven image" commandment removal after seeing demand for their newly created crucifixes.

The Holy Trinity

We believe three Gods exist in one person: the Father, Jesus, and the Holy Spirit. It's a holy trifecta, a set of three equally perfect Gods in their own right. The Holy Trinity can be difficult to explain, and must have been especially hard during the Church's early years considering teachers had no audio-visual aids. God, the Father, and God, Jesus the Son, are easy enough concepts to wrap our minds around. Father and Son. Dad and his boy. Andy and Opie. Got it. But that God, the Holy Spirit, still throws us for a loop. When I was a kid, He used to be called the Holy Ghost. The name change came about after television was invented. Kids were confusing Him with a friendly cartoon character, Caspar.

Saint Patrick was probably the first to discover a teaching prompt, the three-leafed shamrock. Today, the shamrock has become a symbol of another holy trinity: beer, whiskey, and leprechauns. The trinity concept caught on and other not-so-holy trios emerged.

Ten not-so-holy trinities

1. Kentucky Derby, Preakness, and Belmont Stakes
2. Moe, Larry, and Curly
3. Huey, Dewey, and Louie
4. The Bee Gees
5. The Good, the Bad, and the Ugly
6. Hear No Evil, Speak No Evil, See No Evil
7. Three Blind Mice
8. Three Little Pigs
9. Snap, Crackle, and Pop
10. Charlie's Angels

Transubstantiation

Jesus bestowed upon his disciples and future priests the gift to transform bread and wine into His body and blood during Mass. Known as Transubstantiation, this transformation means Jesus is with us physically through His presence in the Holy Eucharist (Holy Body of Jesus). We receive the Holy Eucharist at communion in the form of a "host"—bread (wafer) and wine. It's through this act we literally become "one body with Jesus," giving us strength and motivation to live holy and Christ-like. Other denominations share in communion, believing the act symbolic of the Last Supper. We Catholics get the real deal, the body and blood of Jesus AND actual bread and wine. Everyone else gets crackers and grape juice. Transubstantiation allows us to carry within us Jesus, the bread of life. You can't get that from a saltine.

This should have been one of the toughest beliefs to learn when I was a kid, but, thankfully, we had the nuns teaching us. Keeping it simple and visual, sister after sister taught this belief using simple threats: "Don't chew Jesus or you might break His bones." That was my personal fave. If you chewed, they warned, blood would gush. Not from the bread/wafer in communion crunchers' mouths, but from their knuckles after a sister caught them.

Resurrection

Central to Christian beliefs is the Resurrection where, after three days, Jesus rose from the dead. That fulfills the promise that His death ensured eternity in heaven to believers. This is not at all like when hubby comes home Sunday morning after going AWOL Friday night and promises his wife he's giving her a trip to paradise. God keeps His promise. Hubby, on the other hand, would foist a ferry ride across the Passaic on her if he thought he could convince her paradise lay on the Jersey Shore.

Virgin Birth

Catholics and other Christians believe Mary was a virgin when she conceived and gave birth to Jesus. As certain as we are in this truth, we're just as sure about another. Mary's virgin birth has been the only one. Ever. No one can lay claim to that miracle, no matter how convincingly she tries. Just ask Bristol Palin.

Sin

Catholics, as do other Christians, believe we sin. However, our classifying them as either venial or mortal has some Protestants flipping through their Bibles asking, "Show me where you find that in the scriptures?" I usually tell them it's in one of the books King James tore out. When I really want to mess with their minds, I throw in my "We're the original Christians" argument.

The standard definition of sin is that it's an act where we purposely hurt God by disobeying Him. All Christians can agree on that. However, that explanation cuts a wide swath. For some Christian denominations, dancing is sinful. Yeah, it's easy to see how a Texas two-step can hurt God. Sandals are no match for cowboy boots.

Sinning began in the Garden of Eden when Adam and Eve disobeyed God's instruction to not eat the forbidden fruit. How hard could that have been? It's not as if they were asked to lay off the steak. After committing that original sin, Adam and Eve spiraled downward. First came bickering over which of them was at fault, then public nudity. Finally, they were kicked out of Paradise. Sounds like the first season of *Survivor*. Just like winner Richard Hatch, life got worse for them and for mankind that followed.

After a few millennia, things got so out of hand that God sent us the Ten Commandments, guidelines for sin-free living set in stone. Literally. Even still, sin waters remained murky. Thou Shalt Not Kill might have seemed obvious if you whacked an intruder on the head with a machete, but what if that stranger was a snake meandering through your garden?

Catholic powers that be solved that dilemma by labeling sins as either "mortal" or "venial." Mortal sins give us a fast pass to hell, while venial sins won't keep us out of heaven. Mortal sins are extremely grave transgressions where you knowingly violate God's law in a serious way, like murder, adultery, or sleeping in on Sunday to avoid Mass. Venial covers the rest. Committing a mortal sin is like landing on the Go Directly to Jail square in Monopoly. Venial sins operate like an anti-rewards card that gets punched each time you lie, hit your little brother, or tear up a parking ticket. The more holes on the card, the longer it takes for you to enter heaven.

The good news is we Catholics have Confession. Go to your priest, drop to your knees, and rattle off your sins. Sincerely, of course. Then promise to try and sin no more. Sincerely, of course. You're awarded a Stay Out of Hell card and the chance to start life anew with a clean slate. The challenge is keeping the slate clean. The good news is when we slip off the sin-no-more bandwagon, there's always Confession.

Heaven

Catholics are pretty much in agreement with other Christians about heaven's existence. The ultimate in gated communities, heaven's exact location is unknown, but artists, storytellers, and drunken Irishmen have long portrayed it as upwards in space and filled with clouds. You know you've arrived when you see creatures draped in flowing robes with golden halos topping their heads. These creatures are genderless in a Saturday Night Live "Pat" sort of way. Heaven is illuminated by a bright light and a serene happiness prevails, as well it should. In heaven, you're enjoying God's kingdom, along with its overflowing cornucopia of fruits. There's no illness, no poverty, no hunger. All needs are provided for, including free Internet. Even a Bernie Sanders' America couldn't top heaven.

Hell

Again, Catholics and other Christians are on the same table regarding hell. If heaven is located atop a mountain of clouds, hell is located in the deepest bowels of earth. Walls of burning fires and beds of boiling brimstone mark the entryway to hell, as do a staff of gnarly, withered, scaly attendants. Throngs of near-naked sad sacks shuffle back and forth, moaning and kvetching about their unbearable conditions.

"Oooh, this heat is scorching my skin. Every hair on my body is fried and frizzled. I feel like a Brillo pad. Trust me, not the lemon-scented kind, either. And the service? Don't get me going! You'd think eating in a barbecue we'd at least get shish kabob for dinner."

Never before has humanity experienced such misery. Okay, maybe by early-bird diners in a Boca Raton retirement community.

Mass

Catholics, like other Christians, assemble in a church each Sunday to worship God. If you're a Protestant about to holler, "Do I hear an Amen," and then decide to swing by St. Jerome's Catholic Church because it's closer to home, be aware. We do things differently. By the same token, all you Catholics thinking about slipping into Calvary Hill Baptist Church for the same reason, you know you can't do that. At least you should know that.

We Catholics don't attend Sunday service. We participate in Mass. That's the correct lingo for describing our Sunday worship. Also, we're obligated to attend every Sunday. Skipping Sunday Mass because the Country Club pro-am kicks off at eight a.m. is not an option. Neither is setting your DVR to "Mass for Shut-ins" just because you're hungover. Not being able to crawl out of bed because Bloody Mary bushwhacked you the night before doesn't qualify you as a shut-in.

Purposely missing Mass marks our souls with a mortal sin. By now you can probably guess the repercussions. Yep, you get to checkmark "crispy or extra crispy" on your eternal visa. Fortunately for us, Masses are scheduled several times on Sunday, as well as one on Saturday night. Throw in the fact there's a Catholic Church in nearly every city, and a website sharing locations and Mass times, you've got no excuses to not attend.

My intention is not to diminish the importance and beauty of our Mass, or to be so cheeky that old nuns will drop to their knees on my behalf, but I've come up with a simple way to describe what happens. I liken it to attending a fancy dinner party. Imagine one such soirée at St. Agnes Catholic Church in Any Town, USA:

The Ultimate Dinner Party

We guests arrive at St. Agnes, some early to ready themselves, others rushing through the doors when the dinner bell rings. A few straggle in after the host and his entourage have made their entrance. Once most of us are seated, our host and his servants arrive in a grand procession that's usually heralded by song.

Our host this week is Father McGinty. He's accompanied by his butler, Deacon Miller, and a crew of young footmen known as altar servers. All arrive nattily attired, some wearing dashes of color noting the current Church season, others mixing and matching cassocks. Stoles drape their necks, and cinctures wrap around their waists. Their wardrobe looks as if it came from the same closet. Actually, it did, in a room located in the sanctuary.

Joining them in the grand promenade down the center aisle are liturgical ministers that will read Holy Scripture to us. A cantor, who will lead us in song, joins them. Although not dressed in formal church wear like the others, the ministers and cantor arrive in their Sunday best. The only thing missing from the entrance processional is a red carpet and Ryan Seacrest.

Father McGinty welcomes his guests and reminds us why we are there. And, no, it's not because we risk eternity in hell if we skip. Rather, we come together to receive a special gift from our king, Jesus. The Mass proceeds with scripture readings, songs, a homily, and prayers for ourselves and for special intentions. Next, we share gifts with our host. We present wine, bread, and money that comes from a passing of the plate. Sometimes, we squeeze in two passings. Hey, it's a Catholic church.

With the help of his servers and deacons, Father McGinty prepares the meal, much the way Jesus did during the Last Supper. Father mixes just the right amount of water and wine, then wipes the altar clean. Yeah, I know. No man ever cleans a counter. You'll have to use your imagination. There were no women at that last dinner party. Father then asks if we are ready to join him in the main course.

The big act follows—the consecration. That's where transubstantiation takes place. Father McGinty changes the bread into Jesus's body and the wine into His blood. It's a solemn and reverent occasion, holier and greater than even that Chevy Chase moment before the Christmas turkey is carved. We are all on our knees. Father takes the first bite. He eats the bread that now contains the body of Christ. He then drinks the chalice of blood that amazingly still looks and tastes like wine. Real wine, not grape juice.

From the congregation, a slew of helpers we call Eucharistic Ministers step up to the altar and receive the Body and Blood of Jesus. We are then invited to sip and taste. We walk forward to Father or one of the ministers to receive Jesus's Body and Blood, making us one with Jesus. We carry Jesus within us back to our pews and in our bodies until next Mass.

After dining, there's a bit of housekeeping on the altar. Chalices are wiped clean and leftover consecrated hosts of bread are stored in a special receptacle called the Tabernacle. Guests remain kneeling, men checking their watches and women gaping in awe watching grown men and teenage boys pick up after themselves.

Finally, Father McGinty sends us all on our way with a blessing and instructions to sign up for the annual parish fair committee. He and his entourage proceed back down the aisle and then guests exit. All except hot-rodding dads trying to beat parking lot traffic. They skipped out after communion.

Holy Day of Obligation

Throughout the year, the Church observes special occasions that are celebrated with Mass, which we are required to attend. Some Holy Days are well known, such as Easter and Christmas. Other Holy Days of Obligation leave many of us scratching our heads. To make sure they're not preaching to empty pews, priests often throw out hints at Sunday Mass preceding the Holy Day.

"Next Thursday is December eighth. What do you suppose we have going on that day?" Father Jankowski asks his congregants before administering the final blessing.

Parishioners fidget in their seats, shooting each other nervous glances.

"Annual blood drive?"

"Sock and underwear collection for the nuns?"

"Oil change on the bishop's Mercedes?"

"It's the Feast of the Immaculate Conception," Father says, reminding everyone that it's a Holy Day of Obligation. "Anyone who can tell me what that day commemorates will get a dispensation from attending Mass."

Those Get Out of Mass coupons are as rare as a teenage boy waking before noon and offering to drive his grandmother to seven a.m. Mass. Voices cry out, "Honoring Mary for being a virgin when she conceived Jesus!"

Father sighs. "Does anyone know?"

Rosa and Theresa Giannetti, twin Octogenarians seated in the first pew, say in unison, "Our Blessed Mother was conceived without the stain of Original Sin. Unlike the rest of us wretches."

"I'll see all of you here Thursday," Father tells his congregation, including the Giannettis. They attend Mass every day and wouldn't dream of missing a Holy Day.

Many Catholics are surprised when they learn that the first day of the year kicks off with an official Holy Day, Solemnity of Mary. Because of late-night revelry and day-after hangovers, the only attendees are mothers of New Year's Eve partiers. They like to think of that Holy Day as a solidarity of moms.

Equally surprised to learn Black Friday is not a Holy Day are Catholic bargain seekers holding overnight vigils in Walmart parking lots. Not only is there no obligation to be present when store doors open, there's not even a requirement to step inside. None of this made any difference to sleep-deprived women who hadn't bathed in two days and were standing in line wearing aprons covered in gravy stains. Nabbing the holy grail $19.99 foot massage was in and of itself a religious experience.

Feast Days

Specific days are set aside on the Church calendar to celebrate holy benchmarks, or saint days of honor. Some are Holy Days of Obligation, like All Saints' Day, but others, like the Feast of All Souls (one day later) are not. As a kid in Catholic school, I cherished All Saints' Day. Celebrated November first, St. Luke School closed for the day. Win-win! I scored a free day to snack on Halloween candy and my lucky parents got to take an unpaid day off from work so they could shuttle us to our obligatory Mass. The next day, November second, was still a feast day but we weren't required to attend Mass.

In fact, many feast days not only don't require our obligated attendance, but are so obscure that only a handful of cloistered nuns in New Jersey observe them. Hey, how else would those sisters spend their time—throwing dice in a Trump casino?

Supreme Feast Days

A few saint days are so popular that they're celebrated with festivities ranging from dancing in the street to mosh pit diving Saintapaloozas. Creating most of the hullabaloo are two that occur within days of each other—St. Patrick and St. Joseph feasts.

St. Patrick's Day

Saint Patrick's Day is, undeniably, the king of feast days. Patron Saint of Ireland, herpetologists, and craft beer brewers, St. Patrick is paid tribute by millions every March seventeenth. However, his feast day is not a Holy Day of Obligation. I wouldn't advise sharing that tidbit with someone named Finnegan, O'Rourke, or Cohen (everyone lays claims to Ireland that day).

Even though St. Patrick's Day was removed from the official Church calendar years ago, there is no shortage of merrymaking. The faithful continue to pay homage to the Emerald Isle saint with day-long partying that usually begins at a parade and ends in a pub.

We do have obligations to fulfill on his feast day, which include covering ourselves in green (body paint optional), guzzling dyed beer, and telling everyone we see, "Kiss me, I'm Irish." It's not quite what the Church had in mind, but St. Patrick's Day has become a spiritual experience for thousands of bar patrons.

The Feast of St. Joseph, Husband of Mary

A favorite holiday in Italian communities, the Feast of St. Joseph is celebrated March nineteenth with parishioners piling culinary delights onto a table at the church's altar. Originally created as a show of thanks for blessings of rainfall and fruitful land, St. Joseph's Day has evolved into the Indy 500 of cooking competitions for Italian women. Weeks before, young mothers and nonnas alike whip out aprons and stock-pots, stewing, salting, and stirring 'round the clock in contention for first-taste-by-Father status.

Women cook fava beans, along with treats such as figs and cream puffs. Although they also prepare traditional pasta and sauces, baking sweets takes top priority. The goodies help take the edge off their husbands' Lenten sacrifices. There's only so much a man can give up. Confections are favored parish wide, most notably by cardiologists, dentists, and scrawny women in charge of Weight Watcher weigh-ins. After ladies finish cooking, they spread the food out on St. Joseph's table and step away. Like barflies hearing last call on ten-cent beer night, the rest of the parishioners rush the altar and smash the table to bits. Then, the feasting begins.

Because St. Joseph's feast takes place two days after St. Patrick's, I have a theory about how it took off in America. A motherly call-to-action in Boston's Little Italy boosted what was once a quiet celebration into a cross between *Hell's Kitchen* and *WrestleMania SmackDown.*

The transition took place after young men from St. Dominic Church got violently ill after drinking warm, green beer one St. Patrick's Day. Maybe it was youthful pride or a macho act of bravado that drove them to drink, but the Italian lads had no business slamming back Guinness with the boys from St. Brigid's. They were so far out of their league, even St. Brigid nuns were putting away pints before the boys had a chance to blow foam off their mugs. Saint Dom boys might've stood a chance had the bar served Chianti or Rosé. That happening at Sullivan's Lucky Shamrock Bar was as likely as hearing one of the Irish boys say, "Sure, go ahead and date my sister."

After two days watching their children suffer, the Italian mothers and grandmothers set out on a holy mission to quell those queasy, ale-soaked stomachs. Directing each other like first responders at an oil spill, women came together and cooked a carb-laden feast.

"Nonna Concetta, more oregano!"

"You call that a pinch?"

"More, more, more pasta into the pot."

When it was all said and done, so much food had been prepared that mounds of leftovers remained. They sent their leftovers to the church altar. Every year since, the tradition continues. Worried women cooking for their boys who couldn't turn down St. Brigid's beer and lining the altar table with leftovers. A feast day was born.

Sacraments—Holy Rites of Passage

Sacraments are visible, outward signs of God's grace. They're holy milestones where God showers us with extra blessings to help us keep the faith. Sacraments are public, often showy, rituals that shout out to the world, "Hey, we've got an extra dose of holy holy! Nanny, nanny, boo-boo." We celebrate seven sacraments. They're pretty much a succession of spiritual rites of passage or milestones, like uttering your first word or taking that first keg stand.

Sacraments typically call for wearing resplendent apparel and the use of water, oil, candles, and whiskey. Okay, whiskey only shows up when an altar boy sneaks in a flask under his cassock. Our sacraments are divided into three categories: initiation, healing, and serving the Church.

Baptism (Initiation)

Being the sacrament that officially welcomes us into our Catholic family, Baptism washes away the original sin of Adam and Eve. Their disobedience to God not only kept them out of heaven, but barred the rest of humanity, too. That gives new meaning to "payback is hell."

On the surface, our Baptisms seem to play out much the same as for other Christian denominations. There's the universal water-cleansing-away-sin, acceptance of Jesus as savior before a smiling congregation, and a reception afterward. Naturally, we Catholics have a few different plays in our book.

We don't dunk. Other faiths often baptize by full immersion into a body of water. We pour water over baptizees' heads. I know, I know, St. John the Baptist started the dunking thing in the Jordan River, but the Church took a different route early on. Saint Paul called out for Christians to baptize entire communities, which we presumed to include infants and small children. Maybe after losing a kid or two who hadn't mastered the art of not breathing underwater, Church fathers said, "There's gotta be a better way." They might have tried attaching nose clips or wrapping shrouds over faces, but would have given up that practice, too. Maybe fewer followers drowned, but nearly twice as many probably suffocated. The flock was shrinking, not increasing, so Church leaders set out on a dunk-free path. If you hear a Catholic talk about a dunking after Mass, he's talking about donuts into his coffee.

We don't sprinkle. Some refer to our baptisms as "sprinklings" and claim we aren't truly baptized. They insist the one-and-only baptism takes place through full-body dips in pools, lakes, rivers, and other bodies of water large enough for submersion. Even the wave pool at Holy Waters World works. Added bonus, afterward you can grab a tube and float down the lazy river.

Our baptisms welcome new members into our Catholic community. They call for wearing a white gown or robe, anointing with oil, and lighting candles. This is not to be confused with the welcome northern Catholics (like my parents) received when they moved to the Deep South during the 1950s. Sure, there were white robes with hoods, but instead of oils and candles, some were met with tar and torches.

We normally are baptized as infants. This isn't because we hope babies are too young to register traumatic memories of being squeezed into Grandma Great's christening gown or getting a whiff of Godfather Bert's boozy breath. (A good number of Catholic boys found themselves on a therapist's couch years later, trying to come to grips with breaking out in cold sweats whenever they saw lacy, white gowns.) There's no waiting until a child *decides* he wants to be baptized, the way some Protestant kids do.

It's our Catholic duty as parents to call that shot. Waiting for our kids to tell us when they're ready is as productive as waiting for them to tell us when they're ready to get their flu shot. Traditionally, baptisms took place within a couple days of birth, just in case a baby should die. This way, a baptized baby went straight to heaven. If a child died before he could be baptized, he was sent to Limbo, a heaven-ish home. It had all the comforts of heaven, except for the biggie. No God. How sad is that? Babies floated around in Limbo for eternity, but at least they weren't in hell. That was how it was explained to me. That's like saying, "It may not be the Hilton, but at least it's not a cardboard box." I guess the Church finally figured out God wouldn't want His littlest, most precious ones separated from Him, because we no longer practice that belief.

First Holy Communion (Initiation)

With the pageantry of a *Toddlers and Tiaras* runway walk and reverent pomp of a royal wedding, First Holy Communion invites children to receive Jesus's body for the first time. It's a day when relatives gather, snapping photos and swilling whiskey. And that's before they step inside the church.

My First Communion mirrored that of thousands of other Catholic children that May 7, 1966. Dressed in white, we were signaling our souls were pure enough to receive Jesus's body. I, along with the rest of the girls, wore a poufy dress, ankle socks, patent leather shoes, veil, and gloves. We carried plastic purses large enough to carry our rosary beads and our *My First Mass* books, but too small to carry potential distractions, like a pack of Lucky Strikes. Boys were decked out in white suits, giving them a jump on that John Travolta *Staying Alive* dance craze. All of us lined up to enter the church in a procession, girls in one line, boys in another. Nuns stood in the middle directing traffic.

Our big moment arrived when we knelt in front of the altar and waited for Father to place the Eucharist—the communion host—on our tongues. Back in the day, no matter how pure any of us were, even nuns-in-the-making, we were too tainted to touch His holy body. Above all, "Don't chew Jesus," the sisters told us. Nuns stood on the lookout for munchers, and heaven help them Monday if the sisters found one.

These days, there's still plenty of splendor in a First Communion, but some modernization, as well. In my church, girls still wear white dresses, but veils are optional. Some grandmothers insist on sharing their childhood gloves with their granddaughters, but girls today aren't allowed to wear them. We can now receive communion in our hand and put the host in our mouth instead of having Father place it on our tongue. Granny's fifty-year-old moth-ridden yellowed gloves don't hold up to purity standards for touching Jesus's body. Apparently, uncovered hands that spent the previous hour picking noses do.

The most dramatic changes have been in boys' clothing. They must still wear a white shirt and tie, but just like disco, gone are the white pants and jackets. I think that tradition ended when First Communicants started receiving the Blood of Christ in the form of wine, which wasn't allowed when I made my First Communion. Seeing this as their chance for an early morning buzz, some of the boys guzzled from the chalice. They regretted that move later, standing in the sun for photos with Father. So did Father. After hours of soaking and scrubbing red splotches from white pants and priests' vestments, mothers demanded a dress code revision.

Processions have also changed. Girls and boys are no longer segregated into separate lines and pews. It was only a matter of time. First, there was the Equal Rights Amendment and then Title IX, which allowed girls' athletics programs in schools. Then, with the uproar over transgender bathrooms, First Communion practices were bound to catch up. In addition to mixed procession lines, some churches allow parents and siblings to walk in with their communicants and sit next to them. Gone are the days ditching out a side door to sneak a smoke.

Confirmation (Initiation)

Confirmation is where we accept gifts of the Holy Spirit and proclaim both our allegiance to Catholicism and our willingness to live an apostolic life. This sacrament calls upon young adults to become "Soldiers in Christ's Army." Formerly introduced the year after kids made their First Communion, the sacrament now takes place years later.

It must have dawned on Church leaders that an eight-year-old might not be mature enough to tackle the responsibilities that come with serving in Christ's Army. I'm sure some duties he could handle, like climbing monkey bars after school with neighborhood Protestant kids and trying to convert them with promises of, "You'll love our sweet nuns." But don't be surprised to see him later that night, caving from the weight of his obligations and lounging in his dad's recliner. There he'd be, sipping a Pabst Blue Ribbon, puffing unfiltered Marlboros and muttering, "It's a jungle out there."

Leave it to a group of men who've never raised children to solve the dilemma by pushing back enlistment age to thirteen or fourteen. Teens in the throes of puberty and peer pressure have all the maturity in the world to make adult decisions. That's like dropping your kid off on Bourbon Street and telling him to make good choices. The Church wised up and now Confirmation takes place at the almost adult age of sixteen. Plans are in the works for combining the Sacrament with Driver's Ed classes.

Confirmations are such a big deal that the Church calls in its top guns to preside over them. Although an archbishop occasionally steps in, most are handled by a bishop. His appearance kicks parishioners in get-the-church-grounds-kids-priest-gussied up mode. It's a tactic New Yorkers use when Paul McCartney visits Madison Square Garden.

During the sacrament, each child walks to the altar and faces the bishop. A sponsor joins him, placing his hand on the child's shoulder in what appears to be a show of support. Really, he's propping the kid up for "the slap." The bishop stands before the congregation, prepared to do what every father from Ward Cleaver to Jay Pritchett has dreamed about: wallop a teenager without getting a call from Child Protective Services. In a test of the child's commitment, the bishop strikes the young person's cheek. Okay, that's what my nuns led me to believe. The bishop places his palm on our cheeks in a symbolic suck-it-up gesture. Catholics of a certain age like to recall that act as neither symbolic nor a gesture. Instead, they boast about surviving the bishop's sucker punch. All legend, no fact. At my confirmation, those blows were landed by Sister. Update: in recent years, the rite has been changed, replacing the symbolic slap with a sign of peace. Usually, that means shaking hands but I wouldn't be too quick to rule out a peaceful slap. Or two.

The bishop asks each child what Confirmation name he will take. It once was required to be a saint of your gender, but the rules are relaxed these days. No one raises an eyebrow when a young man steps up to join Christ's Army under the name "Catherine." Don't ask, don't tell. Ours is a modern military.

Kids are allowed to use their birth names, if they prefer. That works well if their parents named them Francis or Theresa, but old-timers choke on their choppers when they hear responses like Ashley or Madison. And for those named Ashley Madison … never mind.

Danielle Schaaf

Reconciliation/Formerly Known as Confession (Healing)

Once we turn seven, the Church says we've reached an age of reason and have stepped over an invisible sin line in the sand. When that happens, we are eligible to receive the Sacrament of Reconciliation, better known in my day as Confession.

One day you're six years old and telling your mom, "I'm not going to eat that crappy Cap'n Crunch."

Mom screams the threat most in my generation heard nightly, "Wait until I tell your father."

You're on your knees that night thanking your guardian angel because Dad gives you a pass. He let it go because the Church says you're too young to sin, even if the word "crappy" back then was on par with today's "shitty."

Pull out that same line on your next birthday, and your dad'll drag you to church to confess your sin. Actually, several sins. In Mike Brady fashion, Dad will list them on the way to church. By the time you arrive, you're ready to confess saying naughty words, disrespecting your mother, wasting food while children in China starve, and thinking naughty thoughts about children in China starving.

Before reaching that age of reason, children were incapable of sinning, or so said the nuns who taught me. This means those nasty neighborhood thugs who stole the money I was saving to buy a Monkees album could have walked away with a clear conscience had they been Catholic. Even after dropping more F-bombs than Lil Wayne in concert, they'd get a pass. That's because the oldest in the bunch was six. In an act of divine intervention, I discovered that the under-age-seven rule doesn't apply to all Protestants, in particular those hoodlums. Their mother was a fervent member of the Assemblies of Spare-the-Rod-Spoil-the-Child Fellowship. Being a member in good standing, there's a strong chance she beat the snot out of them. After the squad car pulled out of her driveway, of course.

62

Holy Bones, Limbo, and Jesus in My Cheetos

Catholic kids, on the other hand, barely blow out that seventh candle before they're hauled off to make their First Confession. Even though you had already 'fessed up to your older sister that you snipped a hole in that weird balloon in her purse, it's not the same. These days, kids make their First Confession sitting in front of a smiling and jovial priest who doesn't look like he's jonesing for a smoke. Kids rattle off sins as if they were asking Santa to bring them a BB gun and drone for Christmas. Boom! Say two Hail Marys and come back next spring.

When I made my First Confession, we knelt in a dark closet and whispered through a screen to Father, sitting in an adjacent closet. We confessed heinous transgressions like pouring milk on the cat. Then we'd be told to pray ten Hail Marys. No twice-a-year trips for us, either. We trekked to the confessional every week thereafter.

Being a little shaky on what's exactly considered a sin, a kid relies on his mom, or in my time, one of the nuns, to help them figure it out. They begin by drilling him on the Ten Commandments. I was taught this exercise was "an examination of conscious." It seemed more like verbal flogging. Here's how it typically went:

Mom: "Have you ever coveted someone's belongings?"

Kid: "What's covet?"

Mom: "Have you ever stolen anything?"

Kid: "Does second base count?"

Mom: "Have you committed adultery? Um, never mind."

Mom: "Did you disobey your parents?"

Bingo! The child now has a sin to confess and trots off to Confession.

Once absolved from his sins, the kid is given a penance to demonstrate his sorrow, and willingness to try and not sin again. Penances are usually prayers, presumably doled out based upon the sins' severity. A youngster just getting the hang of sinning might've been instructed to pray one Hail Mary and one Our Father. Someone older, where sin might be a daily occurrence, like crawling under bed

63

covers every night with a flashlight and a copy of *Cosmopolitan*, could've been assigned two Hail Marys, four Our Fathers, and one Glory Be. For the one-step-away-from-pregnancy-or-prison sin watching *Rosemary's Baby* with a date at the drive-in, (Google alert: "*Rosemary's Baby*" and "drive-in.") teens were slapped with an entire rosary. Twice. To be honest, I always suspected Father spun a wheel and dispensed whatever prayer the needle pointed to when the spinning stopped.

A typical penance handed out centuries ago would have been having a sinner parade through the village wearing a sackcloth. Reactions were similar to that of neighbors watching a woman wearing a cocktail dress and stilettos, ambling down a walkway in a morning-after walk of shame. Peasants lined the streets, stared at the poor sap, and whispered guesses about which sins had been committed.

"Stole a ham hock?"

"Bedded down with the town wench?"

"Took Brother John's goat for a joy ride?"

When it came time for me to confess my sins, penances might have changed, but not public curiosity. After receiving his penance in secret, the village sap in my class would've lumbered to the front of the church, knelt, and prayed his assigned prayers. The length of time spent kneeling in front of the altar was the equivalent of knowing how many streets were walked through a medieval hamlet. Reactions were the same, with stares and whispered guesses about which sins might have been committed.

"Stole money out of the poor box?"

"Called Sr. Evangelist a fat pig?"

Every parish priest who drew the short straw to hear seven-year-olds' confessions probably listened to dozens of variations of how they disobeyed their parents.

"I didn't make my bed when my mom told me to last Saturday."

"I didn't throw my socks in the hamper after my mom told me to pick up my room."

"I didn't bring my dad his Miller High Life."

You get the idea.

Occasionally, there'd be a seven-year-old who would confess he lied. Priests must find it difficult to tell when a child actually told a lie, or if he was lying about lying just so he'd have a sin to report. For instance, "My mom asked me if I finished my homework and I told her yes, but I hadn't," could easily be true. Or the child could have made up the sin so he wouldn't be wasting Father's time. Either way, I suppose, the kid's lying and he gets a penance.

Sometimes it's obvious, like when a child says, "I told the policeman my dad murdered my mother." Other times, not so much, especially if the priest was hearing confession from the next James Patterson:

"The cops dragged my dad off to jail. They shaved his head and made him wear an orange jumpsuit and slippers. My mom couldn't get buried because all my dad's money went to pay for his clothes, haircut, and some evil blood suckers called lawyers. I had to chop her up and put her in ice cube trays in the freezer. You might want to skip the rocks and take your scotch neat next time you visit, Father."

Confessions are private and secret. Your declarations are between you and God, through his agent, the priest. There's no one wiretapping the confessional. It's not a presidential campaign headquarters, you know. No one is snooping around, waiting to hear that you pocketed the waiter's tip that lay on the next table (sin: stealing). No one but you, God, and Father Prendergast are going to know you made matters worse by whipping up that story about a homeless guy cruising tables for scraps and God-knows-what-else (sins: lying and taking the Lord's name in vain).

You'd sleep like a baby, too, knowing Father Prendergast's not going to tell his priest buddies at their Saturday night poker game what a lying tightwad you are. His lips won't be sinking your or anyone else's ship. He could be strapped to a gurney with an executioner nearby ready to inject him with a lethal dose of potassium chloride, and he still wouldn't give you up. He's bound by a code of confessional ethics to not let the world know you're a cheap son-of-a-bitch. Karma, a distant Catholic cousin, will take care of that. The next time you visit the restaurant, you'll discover that "homeless bum" was an amateur photographer. Hanging from the cash register is an eight-by-ten glossy of you stuffing the waiter's $2.75 into your pocket.

Anointing of the Sick/Last/Rites/Extreme Unction (Healing)

The sacrament Anointing of the Sick, formerly known as Last Rites or Extreme Unction, traditionally marks a Catholic's passage from earth. It wasn't unusual years ago for priests to make house calls, appearing by your side as you lie on your deathbed. Father would hear your confession, anoint you with oils, and offer you Holy Communion. Before Father had a chance to fold his stole and pack his candles, you'd be halfway up that stairway to heaven. Now we call this sacrament "Anointing of the Sick." The sacrament is a prayerful call for healing, not necessarily a signal you're boarding that last train out of Clarksville.

Of course, this can be confusing, especially to us old-timers. For example, Gramps comes down with bronchitis, but he's not heard about this new, less scary, version of the sacrament. In walks his parish priest and Gramps thinks he's about to have his ticket punched one final time.

"Ah, good day to ya, Seamus," Father Muldoon says as he greets the bedridden parishioner. "Perfect day for a St. Paddy's Day parade, don't you think? Too bad you won't be marching in it this year," Father says as he heads toward the kitchen. He finds Seamus's eighteen-year-old Jameson Irish Whiskey. "You don't mind if I sip a wee nip, do ya? This won't be touching your lips anytime soon," he says, tossing back a shot.

After several "wee nips," Father Muldoon stumbles into Seamus's room. Father spills holy water everywhere, even over Seamus. The priest cries out, "Ah, the devil of it all!"

"I'm not ready to go," Seamus says, assuming Father Muldoon has initiated the Last Rites.

Seamus throws off his bed covers, grabs his shillelagh and jigs a two-step around his room. "'Tis a beautiful morn! I can make it to the street," he says as he ushers Father to the door. A miraculous healing, for sure.

Matrimony (Serving the Church)

Granted, to many non-Catholics, we appear to have strange customs. Popping up and down like fishing bobbers during Mass or voluntarily giving up drinking Dr. Pepper before Easter must seem odd. But a church wedding ceremony is a church wedding ceremony, right? A man and woman vow before God to love, cherish, and honor each other—even when one flips off the TV seconds before the bachelor hands out his final rose.

All true, but Matrimony is one of our blessed sacraments. This means we get the white dress and veil, attendants and groomsmen, candles, music, Bible readings, and out-of-town uncles checking their watches like any other wedding. Because it's a Sacrament, we also receive a huge dose of grace. Good thing. It takes a lot of grace not to retaliate and turn off the TV moments before the final putt in a Master's play-off round.

Here are a few ways Catholic Matrimony differs:

Music

Catholic wedding music is sacred and liturgical. The Church allows only certain songs to be sung or performed. You'll never see a Catholic bride walk down the aisle to "Here Comes the Bride." Don't hold your breath waiting for her to sashay in to "All You Need Is Love," either. Despite objections from wedding planners and Beatles fan clubs, these songs are not sacred.

On the other hand, you might think you've mistakenly stepped inside Saints and Bull Sports Bar instead of St. Bullard's Church when you hear Notre Dame's fight song. Once you see the kneelers, you know you're in the right place but you might wonder if Father O'Toole has a ten-spot on the Fighting Irish game that day. He's working his lucky Irish mojo by allowing the song during the wedding, you think. According to a man whose daughter walked down the aisle to that school's fight song, here is another example of one of our Catholic loopholes. Notre Dame's "Victory March" is a hymn and considered holy enough to meet Church standards, he explained. It gets a sacred thumbs-up and brides can walk down the aisle to that song. I bet if Father covers the spread, he might allow a reprise.

Every college football fan sings their school's fight song with religious fervor, so it's no surprise that Catholic alumni nationwide are lobbying to classify their university odes as hymns. A shoe-in has to be Texas A&M's "Aggie War Hymn." Dodging shellings and gassings, an Aggie Alum wrote that song while hunkered down in a World War I battlefield trench. You know what they say, there are no atheists in foxholes. You'd have to assume a song created in a war-torn hellhole could only have been inspired by God. Besides, it was called a hymn from the get-go.

One school that doesn't stand a prayer of a chance is the University of Southern California, Notre Dame's archrival. Too many priests were on the losing side of bets in match-ups between the two universities. Besides, it's bad juju to enter a marriage to the tune of "Fight On."

Pre-Cana (Pre-Marriage) Counseling
The Church wants to ascertain couples enter their marriage with eyes wide open, considering they're vowing to spend the rest of their lives together. To that end, the Church requires couples attend Pre-Cana counseling. What probably began casually in the rectory where couples sipped coffee while their priest led them in a "what if?"

game, Pre-Cana counseling has evolved into an analytical process second only to a *Criminal Minds* profiling. Couples must participate in classes and spiritual retreats, as well as take a pre-marriage inventory quiz. Couples dig deep into marital responsibilities and answer questions about family planning, finances, and the type of toilet bowl cleaner they prefer. I can't think of a more apropos way to know your match is made in heaven than learning you both swear by Toilet Wand.

Stipulations

At one time, both bride and groom were required to be Catholic. The non-Catholic dutifully converted. Eventually, the Church loosened up and allowed "mixed marriages," now known by the PC title, "interfaith marriages."

If a non-Catholic marries a Catholic, he no longer is required to convert, but must promise to help raise their children Catholic. What's more, the non-Catholic spouse must agree to chauffeur kids to Mass, Confession, religion classes, and to pull weeds in the rectory garden. If the husband is non-Catholic, he's called on to treat Father to weekly rounds of golf, followed by several rounds in the clubhouse. If the wife is non-Catholic, she must commit to taking Father on weekly grocery shopping trips, topped off with a visit to the liquor store. Her treat. At this point, the non-Catholic gives in and converts. It's all part of the plan.

There's value for both husband and wife being Catholic. I should know, I married a non-Catholic. You'd never know it because he attends Mass with (or without!) me and recites the prayers. He's even mastered the left-to-right shoulder sequence in the sign of the cross. Still, those Protestant waters run deep.

For instance, I came home one day to find him gone and assumed he was jogging on the trails in our neighborhood. However, his gum and iPod were still on the table. I've known him to forget his socks when he runs, but never Trident or Taylor Swift. *Maybe he ran an errand*, I thought. I noticed his car keys dangling from the door lock. I picked up the phone and dialed 911 to report a Silver Alert.

"Hello, I'm looking for an elderly, gray-haired man driving a white Buick Century who's gone missing."

"You just described every man in our database," the telephone operator said. "Except for one old dude last seen walking naked on the freeway."

I looked to see if my husband's jogging shorts were nearby.

Just then, my husband walked through the back door. I told him how worried I had been.

"Did you think I was raptured?" he asked.

Raptured? I was bewildered. Then it dawned on me what my Protestant husband was talking about.

"Isn't Rapture the belief that just before the second coming of Jesus some people will get sucked up into thin air, leaving behind a pile of clothes and personal belongings?" I said, still looking around the room for his jogging shorts. The nuns never mentioned that religious teaching.

The reality behind his question set in. When the day of Rapture arrived, he'd be whisked out of his clothes to meet Jesus, leaving behind all his earthly treasures. Including me. He must've assumed I wasn't to be among the Rapture-chosen.

"I get left behind?" I asked. Damn. I wish I had read those books, or at least watched the movies.

"That's the price you pay for being Catholic and not Christian," he said.

Thirty years after our wedding—my holy sacrament—our interfaith marriage is still a work in progress.

No Divorce

Tammy Wynette must have been under the influence of Catholicism when she came up with "Stand by Your Man." There's no such thing as a Catholic divorce. Sure, Catholic couples split, probably after learning about alternating co-custody arrangements.

That's where Dads get every other weekend with the kids and every other weekend to hit the golf course. However, the Church does not recognize divorce. A judge can dissolve your marriage and award your spouse the home, car, bank account, and kids while leaving you with a mangled fishing pole. In in the eyes of the Church, you're still married.

Catholic vows are everlasting, and I mean that in every sense of the word. Let's say you turn eighty years old and dump your bride for a forty-year-old massage therapist. Not long after, Wifey dies of heartbreak. One week later, you suffer a fatal heart attack as a result of a too-deep tissue massage. The next thing you know, you're both standing hand-in-hand before the pearly gates. Of course, you get extra time in Purgatory (relax, that explanation is coming) after Wifey massages the back side of your head with her hand.

Don't think you're stuck if the man of your dream turns into your worst nightmare. Relax, the Church offers annulment, another one of our Catholic loopholes. Annulment is a process that sorta lets you say your marriage never existed, and then the Church says, "okay by us." Never mind you were married for fifteen years, have three children, a mortgage, and spent a week on a dairy farm mothering eight home-schooled kids in an episode of *Wife Swap*. All gone.

As much of a quick fix as an annulment may seem to be, the process is long and painful. It often takes years and can be costly. Recently, Pope Francis suggested simplifying the procedure. Don't you know there was dancing in the streets of Hyannis Port after his recommendation?

Same-sex Marriage

You're killin' me, Smalls! I can't believe people have actually asked if the Catholic Church approves of same-sex marriages. They must've gotten us mixed up with Episcopalians. Either that, or they're the same folks claiming moon walks were staged and filmed in J. Edgar Hoover's garage. Jeez, it hasn't been that long since the Church finally approved interfaith marriages. The only gay weddings in the Catholic Church are those where groomsmen break out the Schnapps. Oh, right. That's all of them.

Holy Orders (Service to the Church)

Often mistaken as the next step after matrimony, when grooms receive "holy orders" from their brides, this sacrament is actually the rite of priesthood. Like post-nuptial orders, only men receive them. The sacrament comes replete with white robes, candles, and incense. A man throws himself on the ground, lying prostrate in acceptance of the Bishop's orders. Some married men undergo a similar ritual. After a boys night out bowling and binging, a husband staggers home and collapses to the ground in front of his wife. Both the priest-to-be and husband cry out, "Have mercy on me!" One receives a blessing, the other a cursing.

Leaps of Faith

As unusual as some of our beliefs and practices may seem, we've got several that are downright mystifying to non-Catholics and Catholics alike. When I try explaining some of them, I get responses ranging from "You Catholics believe the darndest things," to "You Catholics are batshit crazy!" Whatever. They work for us. And for novelists, filmmakers, and Madison Avenue advertisers.

Purgatory

The late, great Yankee catcher Yogi Berra once said, "It ain't over till it's over." With us Catholics, even then, it ain't over. Upon death, those Catholic souls not heading to hell don't automatically go straight to heaven. For some of the holies, like Saint Pope John Paul II and Bing Crosby, it's a given they boarded the express flight north. For the rest of us, we've got a layover in Purgatory. Trust me, we won't need our skis.

Purgatory has long been viewed as a waiting room where suffering, angst-riddled Catholics bide time before entering God's kingdom. Sorta like sitting in a dentist's office. Based on the sins we've racked up over our lifetime—even those confessed and forgiven—our stay could be as short as ten minutes or as long as a millennium. Since no one has seen an after-life clock or calendar, it's hard to say how long souls rest in Purgatory. You could get mowed down by a Blue Bell ice cream truck and wake up in a warehouse standing in a line behind your Uncle Louie, who died last year, and Mary, Queen of Scots, who's been dead for centuries. There's no word on how people pass the time in Purgatory. I carry a deck of cards in my pocket. Just in case.

The current train of thought is Purgatory isn't a physical place, but rather a state of purification. Think of it as a spiritual night-before-colonoscopy prep. The night before your procedure, you alternate downing quarts of nasty-tasting liquid mistakenly named "Golightly" with camping out on the commode doing anything but "going lightly." When it's over, you feel light, clean, and ready to move on. Same for Purgatory. Almost. You won't have someone in the next room yelling, "For crying out loud, shut that damn bathroom door."

Celibacy

The concept of taking a vow to serve God by remaining sex-free has been around for thousands of years. Yet it still seems to be among our strangest, most unnatural, and incomprehensible practices. It's not as if it's implausible to believe priests and nuns abstain from this earthly pleasure, for "All things through Christ are possible." But to not smoke an after-sex cigarette? Mind-boggling. However, ask any married man of a certain age how it's humanly conceivable to go without sex, and he'll share a knowing nod, yet say in a hopeful voice, "All things through Cialis are possible."

Infallibility of the Pope

Infallibility is one of those precepts most people get wrong, like answering truthfully when asked, "Do I have a big butt?" Many non-Catholics assume we believe that whatever the pope says, goes. That was one of the fears many Americans held when John F. Kennedy became the first Catholic president. Ku Klux Klan members and New York Yankee fans alike thought we were all one phone call away from Armageddon. Doomsdayers painted a disturbing portrait:

A red phone in the Oval Office rings. President Kennedy takes the call.

"Hey, Jack, do you think you could do me a few favors?"

"Sure, Your Holiness. Name them."

"For starters, how about a law requiring every American eat fish on Friday?"

"Done. What else?"

"Maybe go to Confession more often? And lay off the blonde. You know, your birthday songbird?"

"Hmm, that's a tough one. Got anything less complicated on your mind?"

"How about dropping one of those fancy-schmancy A-bombs on Russia? This Communism stuff is getting out of hand."

"Now you're talking. Let me take care of some commotion down in Cuba first, but then I'll get right on it."

Of course, if a pope had this kind of pull, Al Smith would have been elected in a landslide back in 1928. Everyone would have known that within moments of Smith placing his hand on the Bible—the Catholic version—Pope Pius XI would've been in his ear, ordering him to quash prohibition.

Assumption of Mary

We believe Mary didn't die and rot in a grave like the rest of humankind, but was instead "assumed" into heaven. As a thank you for her years of obedience, and living with a son under her roof until he was thirty, Mary was assumed body-and-soul directly into heaven. The Church celebrates Mary's assumption with a Holy Day of Obligation. The Assumption is a favorite feast day of mothers with grown sons camped out in their basements.

Stigmata

Definitely one of our freakiest beliefs, along with the notion that nuns go commando under their habits, is stigmata. That's when blood oozes from non-existent wounds on the bodies of future saints mirroring those of Jesus on the Cross. This was one of the few catechism lessons that captured every student's attention. Except for checking their palms for blood, even fidgety kids sat still in their seats listening to holy tales of bloodletting. Ritalin's got nothing over a good stigmata story.

Miracles

An act created from divine intervention, a miracle is a supernatural sign from God. Belief in miracles is another one of our convictions shared by people of all faiths. From Sisyphus pushing a

Danielle Schaaf

boulder up a hill, to a Chicago Cubs fan expecting to see another World Series win in their lifetime, virtually all of mankind believe miracles can happen. The type of miracles may vary. Some are your answer-to-my-prayer variety, like when a cancerous tumor disappears, or your mother finds the cigarette lighter in your purse but not the condom. Others are spectacles of impossible feats, such as the Red Sea parting, or parking in a handicap spot for two hours without getting your tires slit. Although it can take hundreds of years for a miracle to occur, many take place every day.

It's a Miracle!

A mom in a minivan drives over her husband's golf clubs three times and mashes only the ball retriever.

"It's a miracle!"

Rush Limbaugh strolls down Pennsylvania Avenue hand-in-hand with Hillary Clinton.

"It's a miracle!"

Bill Cosby receives a Lifetime Achievement Award from *Family Circle* magazine.

"It's a miracle!" No, that's fake news.

Exorcism

A young girl channeling her inner Allstate Insurance Guy and spinning her head like a Coke bottle in a pre-teen kissing game may make a captivating movie scene, but it's not a realistic portrayal of a Catholic exorcism. An exorcism is our religious rite that drives away demons or evil spirits. The ritual features a priest packing his usual Catholic arsenal of holy water, oils, candles, crucifix, and prayers. Sure, there are risks. The possessed person might sweat and shake uncontrollably. He may even drop an F-bomb here and there or fall into a dead faint. That usually only happens after Father hands him his bill. Casting out demons doesn't come cheap, especially if it takes Father away from Monday Night Football.

The Church has seen a spike in exorcism requests, coming from parents of teens binging on FX's *American Horror Story.*

Apparitions

Sacred phenomena, apparitions are the supernatural appearances of Mary. Throughout history, devout Catholics living on hallowed grounds in France, Sarajevo, Mexico, and Alabama, have reported visits from our Blessed Mother. These apparitions were remarkable in their similarities: a beautiful woman framed by blinding light, shrouded in blue, carrying roses or surrounded by their scent. Most often, she appeared to children or poor peasants who took on an uphill battle of convincing villagers and clergy they had been instructed to share the lady's messages to the rest of the world. Nothing could create more buzz in a town square than a Mary sighting! Okay, maybe spotting Elvis outside of Las Vegas.

One of the more spellbinding apparition stories the nuns told me when I was a child was about Our Lady of Fatima. She appeared to three Portuguese shepherd children in 1917. Compared to most of the other stories sisters taught us during the '60s, the Fatima sighting seemed like it happened only yesterday.

During her visit, Mary instructed the children to devote themselves to the Holy Trinity and pray the rosary every day. The eldest child, Lucia, advised the other two, her cousins, to keep the vision a secret. Little Jacinta couldn't keep her mouth shut and told her mom. Mom must've been the village mouthpiece because news spread quicker than a YouTube dancing cat video. Mary appeared to the children a total of six times, sharing with them three secrets.

The first secret was a vision of hell, with the promise that the children would never go there. The second was the conversion of Russia. These two secrets were revealed by Lucia decades later but the third remained a mystery until the next century. Mary's final visit to the children ended with the miracle of the sun. In front of thousands of onlookers, the sun changed colors and spun like a wheel. And we thought the Chinese cornered the market on pyrotechnic displays.

As a reward for their dutifulness, Jacinta and her brother, Francisco, punched the golden ticket. They got to die and go straight to heaven not very long after the sun-spinning spectacle. Those teen years are so overrated.

Lucia wasn't as fortunate. She entered the convent and lived until she was nearly 100 years old. During that time, she continued reporting visions of Mary. In one, she was instructed to deliver a letter to Church hierarchy that contained that one last secret message from Fatima. She did so and Church fathers sat on it for more than another half-century. Bookmakers gave even odds the letter divulged either the date the world would end or Colonel Sander's secret herbs and spices. Made public in 2005, the letter recounted a vision foretelling a pope's death. Many believed that was a premonition of the assassination attempt on Pope John Paul II in 1981. Looks like the keepers of the secret could've done a better job beefing up papal security.

In recent years, another form of religious sightings has emerged: visions of Jesus's image in food. Trust me, this is not sanctioned by the Catholic Church. From burnt toast to scrambled eggs, photographic evidence began popping up on Instagram and Pinterest. Almost overnight, the "likes" stacked up like viral pancakes.

The next thing you knew, fifteen minutes of fame and fortune came knocking for a dude and his fish stick savior. One Friday night, the guy's munching on a crunchy Gorton's, pretending he's chomping on a T-bone, when he realizes he's about to bite off Jesus's head! That's *so* not gonna happen. He snaps a photo and uploads it to eBay. About the time an *Eyewitness News* van pulls into his driveway, the online auction ends and he's $500 richer.

Apparently, the most popular Jesus sightings are found in snack chips—especially Cheetos. According to the website Buzzfeed, of the top twenty-two images of Jesus in food, six of them were in snack chips. Two of them Cheetos! Clearly, Frito-Lay hasn't fully grasped the religious marketing opportunities. I wrote a letter giving them a head's up:

Mr. Chester Cheetah, Official Cheetos Mascot

Dear Mr. Cheetah:

Now that you've recuperated from your Chester on the Dresser *book tour, I'd like to interest you in a unique and exciting product expansion opportunity for Cheetos. As I was researching religious images for my current manuscript, I stumbled across a website containing photos of Jesus in foods. Although found in banana peels, pizza slices, and ice cream, most images were discovered in snack chips. Two of the most endearing—Preaching Jesus and Crucified Jesus—were found in your Cheetos!*

Mr. Cheetah, Frito-Lay is sitting on a marketing goldmine. With mounting end-time angst and a republican in the white house, what timing could be better for a new line of Spiritual Chips? You could even create a complementary line of Divine Dips.

Forget about beer pong snacks. Kick off football season with Touchdown Cheesus dipped in Prayerful Picante. Better still, re-issue the chip the following Easter as Risen Cheesus and serve it with Sanctified Salsa. Christmas, roll out Baby Cheesus lying in a manger and paired with Shepherd's Spinach Dip or Holy Hummus.

Think, too, of all the advertising opportunities. Instead of claiming chips are made with "real cheeses," you can say they're made with "real Cheesus." Better yet, if you want to make waves among Catholics, go ahead and use the slogan: "It's okay, chew Cheesus!"

I'm sure with such a huge undertaking, your company might be concerned with quality control. Relax, I know a few elderly nuns who'd come out of retirement and give you a hand. Or crack a ruler over your hand. Your choice.

Eagerly awaiting your response and keeping it cheesy,
Danielle

Danielle Schaaf

Practices That Make Catholics Perfect … Almost

Say a Little Prayer

Aretha Franklin's song title, "I Say a Little Prayer" is an understatement by Catholic standards. Compared to the thousands of our ready-made prayers, pleas, and petitions, Protestant invocations like "Now I lay me down to sleep," or "God Is Good, God Is Great" are chump change. And don't get me going about those DIY versions! Unless created by Oral Roberts, those usually end up as ramblings falling on deaf ears. By the time I learned my multiplication tables, I'd already memorized dozens of devotions, litanies, and other entreaties to get me through a month of thanks, trials, and tribulations. We never get stumped over what exactly to pray for, or when, or how. From the time we step out of bed in the morning and until we crawl back in at night, our day of prayers is laid out for us.

Rosary

Some non-Catholics consider our praying the rosary to be the ultimate of in Mary-before-God worshipping atrocities. To them, this ranks somewhere between adoring false idols and snake handling. In reality, praying the rosary is a contemplative, spiritual practice recalling and meditating on Christ's life. We use a string of beads, an ancient practice, to count off a series of prayers.

The rosary traditionally has been prayed under three different themes called "mysteries." They cover the joys, sorrows, and glories of Jesus's life, death, and resurrection. Not too long ago, the Church added a fourth: the Luminous Mysteries. Maybe because we've become obsessed with zombies, or *Real Housewives* who don't behave like any housewife I know, the Church sensed we could use another holy mystery to reflect upon. Holy fangirl alert: I ADORE the Luminous Mysteries!

Praying the rosary takes the same amount of time as hitting up your local Java Shack drive-thru for an espresso double shot. Twenty minutes with the rosary leaves you calm, floating in a sea of peace. After your Java Shack run, you're wired and buzzing in a pool of caffeine.

Litanies

Short bursts of invocations to God, Jesus, Mary, Joseph, angels, and saints, Litanies go something like this:

Lord, have mercy on us.
Christ, have mercy on us.
Lord, have mercy on us.
Christ, hear us…
St. Peter, pray for us.
St. Paul, pray for us.

Litanies can be recited anywhere and are particularly popular last-ditch invocations. Stuck in traffic? Try the Litany of Divine Mercy. Your recipe for pizza-dough-wrapped pickles has been named a finalist in the Pillsbury Bake-Off? Time to settle in with the Litany of Humility. And for teens coming home two hours after curfew and seeing Dad in the driveway? Rattle off the Litany for a Happy Death, naturally.

Liturgy of the Hours

One of the most beautiful and spiritual praying practices is Liturgy of the Hours. Recited at set times during the day, it's a mix of hymns, scripture readings, and prayers. I think of them as Catholic happy hours minus the half-priced cocktails, appetizers and sleazy pick-up lines.

Novena

When we spend nine days in a row asking the Blessed Mother or a particular saint's intercession for a special intention, it's known as praying a novena. For example, when Grandma can't recall where she's left her car keys and flask, she'll pray a novena to St. Anthony,

Patron Saint of Lost Items. Miraculously, on the ninth day, just as her son starts dialing the phone number for St. Elizabeth's Home for Elderly Moms, Granny finds her keys in the liquor cabinet. Another miracle, Grandma discovers her flask on the car's dashboard. Full, praise be to St. Anthony!

A word of caution. Some items, like Grandma's virginity, can never be retrieved. That calls for a novena to St. Jude, Patron Saint of Lost Causes. A novena to St. Jude comes with a catch. After praying for nine days, we can't just bless ourselves and call it a day. Before St. Jude steps in on our behalf, we've got to give him a shout-out. We're supposed to tell the world we not only asked for St. Jude's intercession, but that we did so day-after-day for nine days straight. Showing up on our neighbor's doorstep and announcing, "Hey, I just prayed to St. Jude for nine days. Got a beer?" doesn't cut it. No, we turn into St. Jude's press agent and publicize the novena through media exposure.

Back in the day, newspapers ran classified sections so Catholics could take out ads glorifying St. Jude's intercession. Ads were placed in the back of the paper, sandwiched between notices of cemetery plots for sale and young mothers seeking new friendships—discretion required. Eventually, laziness and technology kicked in. Instead of appearing in newspaper classifieds, the missive was photocopied. Fliers with news of our novenas were stacked on the ends of church pews, taped to stop signs, and posted to trees. Parking lots were blanketed with "I prayed to St. Jude" notes stuck under windshield wipers. Bet that must've gone over big at the Ida Slutsky Jewish Community Center. With the increasing popularity of Twitter, folks now Tweet the news @Judepatronsaintoflostcauses.

Benediction

Formally known as Benediction of the Blessed Sacrament, this religious ceremony is where the consecrated Eucharist (Body of Christ), in the form of altar bread, is displayed in the center of a cross-shaped mechanism called a monstrance. The Benediction is considered a blessing directly from Christ. This holy, solemn practice dating back to the Church's early years has taken on a twenty-first-century twist with the use of webcams. Churches worldwide offer 24/7 views of the Blessed Sacrament, making it easy to check in on our computers, tablets, and phones. The hope is Benediction will have as many followers as Kingcharlie_doodle on Instagram.

Spiritual Bouquets

Our long-standing tradition of offering a series of prayers for others, known as a "spiritual bouquet," was once a reverent and faith-driven gesture. Spiritual bouquets are now often last-ditch, cheap-ass Mother's Day presents. Protestant moms receive vases filled with peonies, roses, and lilies. Catholic moms get promises of time spent in prayer on their behalf. Right idea, lousy execution. Those promises have the same kind of follow-through as homemade birthday coupons redeemable for washing dishes or massaging Mom's bunions. Being mothers, we continue gushing and pretending to cherish the bouquets just as we did with the scrub brushes, sewing kits, and dental floss that tumbled out of our Christmas stockings.

Way of the Cross/Stations of the Cross

Church walls are adorned with fourteen plaques, photos, or statues depicting Jesus's last days on earth as man. When I was a kid, a Catholic grandma's favorite treat was to surprise her grandkiddies with a stroll. Instead of hiking to the neighborhood park or Baskin Robbins, kiddoes were loaded up in her Buick (that should've been the first clue—who drives to take a walk?) and driven to church. She'd hustle the little ones inside and march them to the first station. There, they'd kneel, pray, and reflect on Jesus's condemnation. They'd move to the second station, Jesus carrying His cross, and do it all over again. Then to the third, fourth, fifth, until they ended up at the fourteenth station, Jesus laid in the tomb. Grandma would usually throw in an extra goodie here—praying a decade of the rosary. Kids found an upside to the two hours they'd spent in church on a Saturday afternoon. They bragged about getting scabbed knees from roughhousing with Grandpa.

Retreats

Catholics gather for periodic spiritual renewal sessions, or retreats. These sessions usually last a day or a weekend, at locations away from home and church. My Catholic gal pals and I relish retreats. They're a lot like our girls' spa getaways, except no one touches you and the massages are mental. After a day of pampering in a spa, we dine on scallops and quinoa salad, washed down with lemon-zested sparkling water. At a retreat, we spend our day fasting and praying, topped off with a brown-bagged sliced cheese sandwich and tap water. All is good. Spa or retreat, there are no dishes needing washing or children banging on our bathroom doors.

Danielle Schaaf

We Got It, So We Flaunt It

We Catholics can be a proud bunch, vices be damned. We undertake practices that are outward signs of our faith and visible proof of our Catholic beliefs. Our pride-on-parade has been around since the days Romans served up Christian entertainment in the coliseums. Just as our forefathers were determined to show Pagans that Christians were made of the right stuff, down to the last gnaw, we Catholics continue their efforts by carrying out practices for all the world to see. It's similar to flashing a two-finger peace sign at the millennial driving her BMW Convertible after she flipped you the bird for driving too slow in the fast lane.

Holy Water

Water blessed by Father and used in all sorts of our religious rites and gatherings is known as holy water. Duh. No one's going to call it unholy water. That's reserved for water flowing from congressional water fountains.

We splash so much holy water around, you'd think every church had its own well out back. We use holy water at nearly every church event and fill receptacles at church entryways with it. We even offer holy water to-go. No drive-thru, though. Yet. Most churches have tanks or cisterns filled with the blessed water so we can pour some into portable bottles and carry holiness home. Clearly, Yeti missed that market.

Every doorway in my childhood home had a water font next to it so we could conveniently bless ourselves. Coming or going, we had a holy spritz at our fingertips. Good thing, too. Who had time to run to church for a holy water blessing when we you headed outside to pick up the newspaper or chase away the neighbor's dog peeing on our porch?

Fonts are still found in Catholic homes, but I'll admit I don't have one at every doorway. I do have one near the back door, doubling as an emergency water bowl for our cat, Sugar. She's outlived all our other pets and is on her eighth life. She can use the extra blessing.

Fasting

The practice of skipping meals in the name of personal sacrifice and cleansing, fasting has much in common with an Oprah Winfrey diet. Both are kicked off with "look-at-poor-me-suffer proclamations" and end with cries of jubilation in between bites of a Big Mac. Fasting has become trendy, endorsed by anti-GMO vegans and catwalk models alike.

Abstinence

Not to be confused with celibacy, abstinence is giving up meat, not sex. We're required to abstain only twice a year, on Ash Wednesday and Good Friday during the pre-Easter season of Lent. Celibacy is not required for married Catholics, but some couples abstain all but two days, typically the husband's birthday and their wedding anniversary.

Kneeling

A systematic self-torture technique favored by nuns and elderly women, kneeling calls for praying on our knees instead of sitting, standing, or God forbid, reclining. The practice is fully endorsed by the National Association of Orthopedic Surgeons.

Genuflecting

A variation of kneeling, genuflecting is how we pay homage to Jesus's presence in our church. Before entering our pew, we bend to the ground on one knee. One innovative woman decided to name them lunges and incorporated them into her workout regime. Genuflect lunges grew so popular that the woman created workout videos, which were bestsellers for decades. It didn't hurt that Jane Fonda looked so fetching in unitards and leg warmers.

Following in Fonda's steps and stretches, other fitness gurus flocked to Catholic churches, hoping to tap into a religious athletic regiment. He'll never admit it, but I understand that soon after Richard Simmons popped in for Sunday Mass, he produced "Sweating to the Oldies." His inspiration surely came from watching nuns hustle up and down the aisles smacking kids on the back of their heads.

Ancient Bells and Whistles
Today's Conventions

Just like modern fitness fiends reverting to the caveman's Paleo diet without much consideration, we Catholics rely on ancient practices and accoutrements without giving them a second thought. (Had dieters thought it through, they might have questioned why cave dwellers died in their twenties.) Catholics learned early on not to question, motivated by the desire to live beyond their twenties. Heretics and Neanderthals shared a common lifespan.

Some are ingrained in us, integral to our rites and rituals, like slipping Father a sawbuck after he gives a two-minute eulogy at Cousin Larry's funeral. Others are mementos we hold dear, out of homage to our Catholic heritage, and because we hope to earn a few bucks in a yard sale.

Holy Oils

Anointing with blessed oils is a sacred practice dating back to the Old Testament. Olive oil has been used for thousands of years in our rites, but these days the Church is testing variations for newly emerging rituals. Recipes under consideration include adding a pinch of lavender for the Rite of Revered Rubdown, and a bit of chamomile for Angelic Aromatherapy.

Because olive oil has grown popular as the "healthful fat," its use has skyrocketed in recent years. Worries loom over a potential shortage. There's talk of switching to Johnson's Baby Oil, but a suggestion the Church use Quaker State got a quick thumbs-down. Rumor has it a group of southern Catholic women rallied for Crisco, but that sizzle never left the frying pan.

Bells

Bells are Catholic musical carrier pigeons, ringing cues and messages to parishioners from church towers and altar servers' grimy hands. A church tower Carillion reminds us that our butts should be

89

planted in pews, not listening to Howard Stern on Sirius XM in the car. Sanctus bells ringing from the altar during Mass alert daydreamers to snap out of it because transubstantiation is about to take place. Those bells also signal approval for dads to rap snoozing teens on the back of their heads so the kids don't sleep through the most important part of Mass.

Candles

Candles in a Catholic church are like Alec Baldwin on *Saturday Night Live*. It's a guarantee that both will be always there, and only rarely do they burn out or blow up. Of course, a Baldwin blowout hits the cover of *National Enquirer*. Candles are simply replaced. Originally used to light dark caverns when early Christians were forced underground, candles now are ever-present. Those glowing illuminators are as much a part of our Catholic life as Snapchat is for teenhood.

One candle holds a spot of prominence in each church. Placed next to the Tabernacle (Don't worry, I'll explain later) where the body of Christ resides, its flame is eternal and reminds us Jesus is present with us always. Nowadays, flames more likely come from battery operated red lights instead of fiery wicks. Not all churches experienced a smooth fire-to-glow transition. A number of parish holy-above-all-others in certain city districts broke out in a sweat when they saw the lights. Seeing the flickering red lights, some parishioners flashbacked to past visits they had made to red-lit doorways of a different nature.

Crucifix

Depicting Christ's death, a crucifix is a figurine of Jesus nailed to a T-shaped cross. It's a visual reminder of how greatly He suffered for us. Although crucifixes are found on church altars, in Catholic schoolrooms, or dangling on a chain from our necks, the most effective reminders are those found in our homes. Step inside a Catholic's home and you'll be greeted by a crucifix. Maybe even two.

Inside my childhood home, nearly every room was adorned with a crucifix. Good Catholic mothers made sure their homes were laden with them, even managing to incorporate them into their home décor. And without the help of Chip and Jo!

For example, in a traditional living room, Rosa Tarramissimo might have placed a handcrafted, wood-carved import from Italy on her coffee table. Odesta Mae Wilkerson (a convert—no cradle Catholic would name their child Odesta Mae), whose den had a shabby chic vibe, might have draped burlap around her crucifix.

When I was a child, a plastic glow-in-the-dark version hung from my bedroom wall. Some of us needed reminding day and night. So impressed by how mindful we kids were of Jesus's suffering, many moms placed photos of themselves next to their children's crucifixes.

Although plain crosses are popular among Protestants, the same is not true for Catholic crucifixes. Reasons vary. There are those who shy away from pain and suffering, instead opting to participate in feel-good ministries where the biggest hardships are finding replacement Oakley sunglasses. Others fear hanging a crucifix on their wall, or worse still, from their necks, will land them in our idol-worshipping camp. I find it fascinating how displaying a replica of Jesus nailed to a cross can be considered idolatry, yet draping a University of Alabama flag over a photo of Paul "Bear" Bryant on game day is not. Go figure.

Holy Medals

If wearing a chain necklace with a crucifix nudges me closer to eternal flames (in the eyes of some), then outfitting myself with holy medals might be the final push into Satan's fire pit. Our holy medals are medallions portraying images of saints. Making sure I never climb out of that literal hell-hole would be my wearing a medal containing a relic. Relics are holy pieces and bits of saints' clothing or bones. Talk about stirring up the graven-image idolatry pot! Most relics were dug up centuries ago, most probably in rituals overseen by Church leaders. I can only imagine how they shelled out grave-digging duties:

"Brother Boniface, grab your shovel and meet me in the monastery graveyard."

"Ah, it can't be my turn so soon," Brother said. "I thought finding the Assisi Sisters in the same grave would buy me a fortnight before my next turn."

"Finding St. Agnes buried alongside her sister, St. Clare, was a rare treat, indeed. Daily doubles are hard to come by," Bishop Albert said. "But we've had a run on bone bits, with that nasty Black Death bug going around."

I've pretty much given up wearing holy medals, especially those containing relics. Sure, I can move beyond the ick factor of wearing bones from some dude who died centuries ago in what was probably a gruesome death. The germaphobe in me can't get past potential health hazards. I bet I'm not alone. Name one person who'd willingly wear a medal with a smidge of St. Aloysius Gonzaga's skin on it after learning he died from the plague. Having a university named after you can't wash away that stigma. Not even one with a championship basketball program.

Besides, it gets old trying to explain why you're wearing some guy's bone chip around your neck, even if it resembles a sapphire. One minute, the cashier checking out your groceries mentions how unique your necklace is, and after you tell her it's a piece of St. Peregrine's rib, she's on the store mic, "Code Dahmer, register seven." Telling her the piece was blessed only worsens the situation. So were the skulls in Jeffrey Dahmer's freezer.

Truth be told, the main reason so many of us no longer wear medals is because we no longer have nuns around handing them out to school kids. Back when sisters in classrooms were as common as black and white TVs in living rooms, nuns routinely rewarded us kids with holy medals. Carrying around a chunk of St. Lawrence, especially if your name was Larry, was almost as impressive to Catholic kids as watching our moms smoke an entire pack of Winston's during one episode of *Bonanza*.

The same thing can't be said for public school kids. No matter how much they crowed over worksheets covered in stickers, even they realized a bone sliver from a 1,000-year-old martyr burned at the stake trumped gold stars.

Holy Cards

While the best and brightest Catholic school kids received medals and statues from the nuns, the rest of us got holy cards. Think Catholic version of Pokémon or baseball trading cards. Each one presented a saint's image on one side and a prayer on the other. Instead of reviewing saintly stats or reciting prayers to help us on our heavenly path, we collected them so we could trade them.

Most holy cards, like most baseball cards, were never worth more than the bubble gum that came with them. Strike that. Holy cards didn't come with gum. Either that, or the nuns took the gum out of the packages before distributing the cards.

Occasionally, a kid got a lucky card. Like Mickey Mantle's card valued at no more than five cents his rookie year, but then soaring in value decades later, a Saint Francis Xavier prayer card did the same. Saint Frank's card didn't fetch $500 million like The Mick's, but having a $500 price listing on the holy card exchange was exorbitant.

You don't have to be Milton Friedman (Google alert: "Milton Friedman") to figure out why there's wasn't a market for holy cards. Supply and demand. Every kid owned hundreds, courtesy of nuns cleaning out their desks and cheap relatives tucking them inside First Communion cards instead of cash.

Scapular

A piece of fabric worn around our necks like a saint's medal, a scapular is a sign of salvation and offers protection from dangers. I was told by nuns that if we died while wearing a scapular, we'd go straight to heaven. Scapulars were never to be removed. Hormonal teenagers tangling in the backseat of a car would've taken Sister's words to heart. Even if they had shed every other piece of fabric in less time than it took to say, "Saint's Begorrah," their scapulars would remain intact. Scapulars may have saved teens from the fires of hell, but were of little protection from the hellfire of a father banging on that car window.

Palms

Oversized leaves traditionally used to fan nobility, palms were waved in adoration of Jesus the week before His crucifixion. Palms are distributed to congregants at Mass the Sunday before Easter, officially kicking off Holy Week. We wave them in the air as Father walks throughout the church, sprinkling us with holy water and blessings.

Not long ago, Canadian Cardinals pushed to replace the palm with another leaf. After hearing the Canadians' suggestion, Italian Cardinals nearly upchucked linguini on the pope's slippers. The recommendation of Maple Leaf Sunday was summarily dismissed. Of course, Oregano Sunday didn't get enough votes, either. The pope called a truce and the Church stuck with palms.

During my tenure in Catholic school, we were taught to leave Mass with our palms intact and place them in a spot of holiness in our home. Every year, my dad folded his palm in half and tucked it behind the crucifix hanging over our front door. As an adult, I followed suit, tucking the palm behind the crucifix in my bedroom every year. That is, until the year my cleaning lady stuck it in her broom, thinking it made a great bristle to get into tight corners. And no, she wasn't Catholic. Since then, it resides atop my jewelry box. Not exactly a shrine, but at least no one is looking for replacement broom parts there.

Some kids got away with bending their palms by shaping them into crosses. In fact, some of the sisters taught kids how to twist and fold the reeds into pocket-sized crosses. Sisters figured they could either teach them how or pick those palms out of the school trash cans.

Crosses were pretty much the extent of our Catholic palm origami. Creating anything else could land us extra time in the confessional. In rare circumstances, a lucky kid might get away with a headpiece, if he said it was a crown of thorns he'd be wearing in the school passion play. Gaining approval to create a Robinson Crusoe hat was a lost cause, even if your family planned to spend Easter at the beach. *Especially* if your family planned to attend Easter sunrise services at the beach. Trust me, sunburns would be the last of your worries if the nuns caught wind of you not celebrating Easter Sunday Mass in church. And asking to create a doll, even one named Sister Mary Regina? Not a chance. These are holy palms, not corn husks.

Ashes

Even though I once worried if those gritty smudges Father smooshed on my forehead the first Wednesday of Lent were the cremains of a stray dog that stole his newspaper, I eventually learned the ashes came from last year's leftover palms. My altar boy buddies told me they burned them in the parish's annual carnival bonfire, along with what looked like Father's old speeding tickets.

Ashes are visible signs in our belief that we begin and end our lives in the same fashion: "Ashes to ashes, dust to dust." To non-Catholics, our darkened foreheads are visible signs we face-planted into the ground trying to snag Mardi Gras beads the day before. Our foreheads make instant icebreakers from countless strangers letting us know we've got dirt on our faces.

Ever since the Vatican II Council in the early 1960s, lay ministers have been ordained to help distribute ashes. If the mark is the size of a half-dollar with a clearly defined "T" and black dots speckle your glasses or nose, the ashes were administered by a lay person. If it's a blob that looks like a fingerprint that would accompany a mugshot, the ashes came from Father. Cross or blot, it all comes down to a numbers game. Priests have developed an efficiency that gets ten people dusted for every smudge from a lay minister.

Vespers

Not to be confused with vapors—the mysterious Victorian ailment that sent women crumpling to the ground in a dead faint—Vespers are evening prayers giving thanks for the day. If you're taking in a Vespers, don't expect to zip in and out as if you're buying lotto tickets at Thelma's Food Emporium. Vespers begin with a hymn, and includes a series of psalms and responses, scripture readings, prayers of intercessions, and the Our Father. The night concludes with more prayers and dismissal.

I recall an urban Catholic school legend where an altar boy passed out during one especially long Vespers. The pastor was on vacation, so the church pulled in a sub from St. Dymphna's Old Folks Home for Frail Fathers. Ever since *Sanford and Son* went into reruns, the guy had nothing better to do on a Friday. He kept the prayers coming and the boy keeled over. No one ever said if the boy was wearing a tight corset under his cassock but, hey, it was the '70s.

Pomp it up!

If you've ever attended a Catholic Mass, wedding, or even a funeral, you know we're big on pomp and pageantry. Dating back to when Jesus walked on water, combining spirituality with spectacle is a crowd-pleasing tradition we can't shake. And we don't want to, either. In fact, it's probably written in our doctrine that we ascribe to "Puttin' on the Ritz."

Processions

It's easy to spot Catholics heading into crowded public venues like Wrigley Field. We're the ones standing back so the high and mighty like Bill Murray or Vince Vaughn and their entourages can enter first. Then we form a procession and walk single file into the stadium, waving Cubs banners, chanting and singing. Like ducklings waddling in a straight line behind momma, we walk in processions because it's imprinted in our Catholic DNA. Whether attending a wedding or funeral, or even entering a school bathroom, we had ingrained in us the art of making a grand—yet, orderly—entrance.

Santo Día Festívo

Some of our Catholic celebrations take pomp and pageantry to an entirely new level. A great example is the Feast of Our Lady of Guadalupe. Commemorating our Blessed Mother's appearance to Mexican peasant Juan Diego in the sixteenth century, some parishes honor her with processionals, prayers, hymns, reenactments, and even festivals. Parishioners don't sit back in the pew and watch. They go all out, from dressing in traditional Mexican attire to topping off festivities serving homemade tamales.

More and more parishes are celebrating this feast day, probably, in part, because of the opportunity it gives them to embrace and share Hispanic cultural traditions. Community members applaud the move. After watching pubs rake in big bucks on St. Patrick's Day, local bar owners are hoping for the same. Time will tell, but one thing is for sure, their petition to the Vatican to name Cinco de Mayo a feast day is dead in the holy water.

And the Crown Goes to…

The grand poobah of processions in my day was the annual May Crowning. That's where we ceremoniously coronate Mary, Queen of the May, after marching around church grounds singing her praises. To many of us schoolgirls, this was our chance to compete in a Catholic Miss America-ish pageant. We didn't parade in swimsuits and the winner got to crown a statue of Mary instead of being crowned. With the nuns in charge, our pageants went off without a Steve Harvey hitch.

You-Catholic-heathens-will-go-to-hell crusaders had a field day with May Crownings. We were double-dipping into the heresy pot by worshipping both a statue and Mary. Even ugly taunts from cars driving by our procession couldn't lessen my devotion to this event. It was the one day we girls in the seventh and eighth grades were allowed to wear a dress to school instead of our uniform. White, of course.

Our procession began in front of our church, St. Luke, and we walked throughout the church grounds. We passed our classrooms, the convent, and even cut through the parking lot in a procession carrying flowers and singing. Leading us were our parish priests, altar servers, and the "Appointed One."

One fortunate girl was chosen each year to coronate the statue of Mary with a crown of fresh flowers. Classmates and parishioners sang verses from "Hail, Holy Queen" as she delicately placed the floral wreath on top of Mary's head. The Appointed One wore a white dress like the other girls, but hers might even be a gown. A veil might top her head. Not exactly a Bert Parks moment, but as good as it got for a thirteen-year-old girl who might one day end up in a convent. Crowning Mary was an honor every Catholic girl wanted bestowed upon her. That, and having Mother Superior ask her to raise a red flag when the hair over Mother's lips started looking like Father's.

The crowning honor only went to girls and probably still does. Despite gender playing less of a role in selecting homecoming and prom queens these days, Catholic boys have as good a chance of crowning Mary as they do of wearing a white gown and veil anywhere other than a costume party. Even then, it's iffy.

Choosing the right girl must be an overwhelming task, especially for the nuns from my era. They had so much riding on the line! Pick a girl who would one day parlay that experience into dancing topless in front of spring break frat boys and you'd have to turn in your habit. I bet many nuns held competitions. Maybe some in the vein of hallowed hunger games, requiring grueling feats that ultimately left one girl standing.

Contests could've been objective, like Marian fact or fiction quizzes. For example, fact or fiction: the owner of Mary's Massage and Nail Salon is a direct descendent of the Blessed Mother. Naturally, we'd know this was fiction. Everyone knew Mary was from the Middle East, not the Far East. There's a strong chance girls today could get tripped up and answer "fact," thanks to *The Da Vinci Code*.

Other competitions could've been more subjective, such as choosing a girl whose father owned a florist shop. Nuns recognized a twofer when they saw one.

Regardless of the format, dozens of girls competed each year and prepared for every aspect of the procession and crowning. They practiced pacing, adjusting the length and speed of their steps. Girls knew no one wanted to sing, "Immaculate Mary, your praises we sing," only to find themselves standing in front of the statue with three stanzas remaining. Awkward! Worse yet, think of the poor girl whose procession posse couldn't match her pace. There she'd be, speed walking around the church grounds, through the parking lot, and up the driveway. Once at the statue, she'd turn around and find the entire procession yards behind her, including Father and the altar boys. Like racehorse Silky Sullivan so focused on the finish line, she'd have come from behind and pass Father and the boys, leaving them in her dust.

Poor pacing could be a huge problem for parents joining in the procession. If too quick, by the time the procession reached the statue, the last strains of singing would be drowned out by coughs and wheezes. Most parents smoked back then and had never heard of the Surgeon General, much less his "Danger, Will Robinson!" messages about cigarettes. If too slow, half the dads dropped out when they reached Kingpin Bowling Alley. They would've had enough time to throw a few frames and make it back before the crown touched Mary's head.

A girl's smile played a huge role in the selection process. Hours flew by as wannabes stared into bathroom mirrors wondering if they should go with a pious, pursed-lip or an honored-yet-humbled flash of teeth. Honestly, their ponderings were for naught. The decision was already made for them. If she wore braces, she pursed her lips. If not, she flashed her teeth.

Just as Miss America winners are judged not only on poise, grace, and beauty, but also by how well they answer interview questions, so it was for the girls vying to crown Mary. I was never in contention, due to my un-Mary-like lack of obedience. That, and for calling Sr. Veronica a creep. However, I'm sure my girlfriends must have gone through something like this:

Nancy, the first contestant, steps forward and faces Mother Superior. She represents St. Mary Magdalene's after-school, eighth grade CCD class. Mother looks her up and down. Backstage, Mother had told the other sisters she was determined to figure out if little Miss Drew was the brains in that class of public school brawn responsible for St. Mary Mag students' missing paperwork.

Drawing on her years watching *Jeopardy*, Mother brought out her announcer voice and asked, "If our Blessed Mother could speak to you now, what might she ask of you after you enthrone her statue with a crown of flowers?"

"To serve others," said Nancy, adjusting the Sodality of Mary Society pin on her sash.

"And your response?" asked Mother Don Pardo.

"I'd tell our Blessed Mother I'd volunteer by serving Lenten Fish-on-Wheels to the homeless."

Mother Superior nodded in approval, even though she knew a public school girl's chance of crowning Mary was as slim as a supermodel's waist. Especially one named Nancy. Which saint was that? Still, if Nancy was chosen, Mother was off the homeless-feeding fishhook and could watch *The Mary Tyler Moore Show* with the rest of the nuns. Mary had spunk. Mother Superior loved spunk.

"Most chaste Mother of God would ask me to remain pure," Agnes, the second contestant, answered as she crossed her knees. As president of St. Mary Mag's Virgin Friends Forever—VFF—Agnes added, "I'd take the ultimate step and become a nun."

Mother Superior fist-pumped the air and mentally checked recruiting off that week's to-do list.

The final contestant, representing St. Mary Mag's Rosarians, Mary Elizabeth Catherine said the Blessed Mother would instruct her to "bring flowers of the rarest." Adjusting her veil, she added, "I'd have my dad donate South American roses from his florist shop."

Mother Superior beamed. The deal was sealed. Maybe now Father would lighten up over last year's plastic daisies Katy McDougal brought in from McD's Eternal Peace Funeral Home.

You Know We Must Be Catholic When …

As if we don't have enough Catholic rituals, rules, and requirements, we've created unofficial practices you won't find in our catechism books, like backing into church parking spaces so we can get home from Mass thirty seconds sooner. One common thread many of these acts share is how they draw attention to Catholicism in an "I'm chosen, you're not" kind of way.

Sainting Our Children

When we marry, we pledge to raise our children Catholic. This means making sure they receive their sacraments, attend Mass every Sunday, and learn to head to the water fountain right before the usher reaches our pew with the collection plate. Naming your child after a saint is not required, but practiced by my parents, grandparents, and countless generations before them. I guess the thinking is, if you give the kid a holy name, he'll live a holy life. Yeah, that works just fine. Ask Terese Guidece, New Jersey's real-housewife-turned-real-convict. Or Mr. and Mrs. Ciccone. Had they known their baby girl, named in honor of the Blessed Mother no less, would one day perform a music video banned by the pope, they might have named her Bertha instead of Madonna.

Not as prevalent now, saint naming had been the unwritten rule until about the mid-twentieth century, back when it took longer to get into a Saturday matinee than it did a confessional. So consumed by the burgeoning movie industry, parents started naming their kids after actors more likely to portray a saint than actually become one. At one point, there were more boys name Marlon than Martin.

During the 1950s, the pinnacle in saint names emerged when a young actress graced movie screens nationwide. Although it wasn't until the next decade that Debbie Reynolds actually played a nun, she had become known for portraying sweet, loving, perky, and (mostly) virtuous characters. Apparently, she was saintly enough for Catholic parents because by the mid-sixties, there were more little Debbies in school desks than in lunch boxes. My own seventh grade class of forty students boasted five.

The 1950s Debbie-naming revolution spurred an even more massive rebellion. Names like Ashley, Heather, Bradley, and Roger started showing up on birth certificates. Heaven help us all—the insurgency didn't end there. By the twenty-first century, our saint-naming nail nearly pounded into the coffin when Neveah ranked among the top twenty-five most popular girl names in 2010. No, it's not Irish as some Protestants (most likely those envious of our saint-naming tradition but just can't bring themselves to stoop that low) would have you believe. Not quite. Neveah is heaven spelled backward.

At that point, the saint-naming dike crumbled. Out flowed a waterfall of unsaintly names. Goodbye Agatha, hello Yloh. That's holy spelled backward. An added bonus, Yloh is gender-neutral. It works for girls, boys, the undecided, and those who change their minds down the road. Other names gaining traction are YOLO (you only live once) and LOL (laugh out loud). Although not exactly religious, YOLO and LOL do have an inspirational appeal, in an Osteen-ish sort of way. Plus, they're easy to text.

Saint naming nearly went to proverbial hell in a handbasket with the click of a TV remote control button. A reality show family of big-haired, big-bootied, big-bosomed women became overnight pop culture sensations. Parents did their best to keep up with the Kardashians. Since most didn't have the K's wealth or fame, parents settled for naming their daughters Kim, Kourtney, and Khloe.

I'm hopeful the pendulum is swinging back in the other direction, with naming children after present day saintly role models Pope Francis and Princess Kate. Gotta admit, I've done my part over the years. My children are named Andrew Phillip, Alexander James, and Catherine Elizabeth. It doesn't get more saintly than that.

Non-Catholics Named After Saints

Once non-Catholics saw saint-name successes like dragon-slaying George Clooney and stone-me-to-death Stephen Colbert, they jumped on our give-your-kid-a-holy-name bandwagon. Results have been mixed.

If it works for them, it can work for us
Matt Damon
John Legend
Angelina Jolie
Luke Bryan

Or maybe not
Monica Lewinsky
Edward Snowden
Chris Brown
Michael Vick

Holy Home Decorating

One look inside my childhood home and you could tell by our décor we were Catholic. Crucifixes hung over our doors and every bedroom had a holy water font. A porcelain statue of the Blessed Mother sat on my dresser a holy cards lined the top of my father's chest of drawers.

Back in the day, Catholic parents often used religious artifacts as tools for creating teachable moments. Take the Sacred Heart of Jesus statue, for instance. Many parents found placing it on top of their TV sets created more holy gazing hours for their kids than if it were sitting on a bookshelf. Nicknamed by us kids as "Open Heart Jesus," the figurine depicts Jesus holding open His robes and pointing at His heart. The heart is wrapped in a crown of thorns with flames shooting out of it. Resting on top of the TV sent a clear message: watch too many episodes of *Dark Shadows* and you'll spontaneously combust. Some Protestant parents admired the top-of-the-TV scare tactic and gave it a try. As frightening as it was, a photo of Richard Nixon raising his arms in a victory salute didn't quite measure up to a pierced and flaming heart.

Like naming our children after saints, this un-dogmatic tradition of decorating our homes with Catholic adornments has seemed to fade, or at least been minimalized. In my own home, we have one crucifix in our living room and a holy water font made of wood that leaks water. In my office, there's a small statue of Jesus preaching to Martha and Mary propped next to the "You Can't Scare Me, I Have Children" plaque on my credenza. A four-inch plastic statue of the Blessed Mother sits on my window sill, along with photos of my children. I consider that spot my shrine to motherhood.

Outside is another matter. Drive through a neighborhood and you can identify which homes belong to Catholics by their lawns. Count on finding a St. Francis statue, Patron Saint of Animals, under a shade tree in a Catholic's yard. Under St. Frank's outstretched arms, you'll probably see a menagerie of ceramic bunnies and squirrels. Maybe even an alabaster deer or two. Of course, these days, you'd likely see an army of collegiate garden gnomes standing guard around the good saint and his critters. All from various St. Francis universities, of course.

Peak around the corner of the house and there's a good chance you'll discover a bathtub shrine to Mary. Long before there was Pinterest, when our decorating inspiration came from daydreaming and visions, one crafty Catholic saw potential in an old, discarded bathtub. He cut it in half, placed it upright on his lawn, and placed a statue of Mary inside. Voilà! He created a personal grotto where he could enshrine Mary amid a spray of fresh flowers and a ring of not-so-fresh soap scum. Nothing pays homage to the Mother of God like a ring around the tub.

A warning: if you check out my lawn for proof of my Catholic identity, you won't find any. Not a statue, not a door wreath, not a wind chime. Nothing says, "Hey, Catholics live here." That's because of an interfaith marriage compromise. When we bought our first home, I asked my husband, our landscaping guru, if we could put a statue of St. Francis in the front yard. His response?

"I agreed to raise the children Catholic, not the lawn."

To this day, our lawn decorations are decidedly nondenominational.

A Guy Steps into a Catholic Church

A church is a church is a church. Not when it's a Catholic church. The basics are the same— hard wooden seats, dim lighting, and Vegas-style sound systems. We toss a few extras into our churches, which can leave visitors bewildered. It's not enough that we confuse them with our rituals, like making them stand, kneel, sit, and repeat. Visitors walk through liturgical landmines as soon as they enter the church.

Holy Water Fonts

There's no getting in and out of a Catholic church without dipping fingers into a water-filled cup mounted on a wall or in a huge basin in the middle aisle blocking the doors. They're like TSA checkpoints, without X-ray screening machines and scowling sentries keeping watch.

Tabernacle

Usually ornate and locked, the tabernacle is a container on the altar that houses consecrated communion hosts between Masses. The tabernacle is what we're supposed to gaze upon when we genuflect, not the new organist who is the spitting image of Billy Joel.

I've never seen the inside of one, but since Jesus lives there, I imagine it's well appointed. The lighting is cozy and the walls are made from tufted velour. Wait, wrong home. That's the bottle in *I Dream of Jeannie*. I'm sure Jesus's home is much nicer, with recessed lighting, surround sound, and an Amazon Echo.

Statues

Probably nothing is more associated with Catholic churches than statues. I consider statues visual prayer prompts that help Catholics, especially children, reach a meditative, reflective state. They're surely more effective than listening to Tinky Winky jibber and jabber to

Dipsy, Laa-Laa, and Po. Admittedly, a Teletubby trance does come close.

Which statues a particular church showcases often depends on how old the church is and who it's named after. It seems every nook and cranny in an old church houses a saint's statue, while newer ones will have as few as two—Crucified Jesus over the altar, and a statue of the Blessed Mother.

The statue of Crucified Jesus is life-sized and towers over the altar for all of us to see the instant we walk inside. The agony and suffering of his death is clearly depicted. If that doesn't get you on your knees pleading for mercy, I don't know what would. Okay, maybe hearing your mother say, "Hand me the belt."

"The Times They Are A-Changin'"

Danielle Schaaf

Back to the Future

After centuries of observing the same-old routine, the Church has undergone dramatic changes over the last fifty years. Many are returns to early Church practices, such as calling for our priests to face their congregations during Mass, or saying Mass in our native tongues instead of Latin. Other changes may have looked like a spiritual revolt to some, such as allowing women on the altar during Mass. Still, some are kindhearted necessities, such as allowing mentally challenged congregants to receive their sacraments, or serving gluten-free hosts to celiac sufferers.

As our Church continues to grow and reach out worldwide, I believe we will see even more inclusionary improvements in the next fifty years. However, here are a few developments I'm pretty sure won't happen, at least not in (what's left of) my lifetime:

1. Coed rectories
2. An uptick in construction of convents
3. The Vatican relocating to Las Vegas
4. *Holy Bones, Limbo, and Jesus in My Cheetos* landing on the pope's reading table.

Author's Penance, er, Note

If you've made it this far, you've figured out my take on the Church is irreverently reverent. Or reverently irreverent. Whatever. However, nowhere have I purposely veered from Church teachings, but, as admitted upfront, my explanations are theologically thin. The Nicene Creed, created about 300 years after Jesus's death and recited at Sunday Mass, is a great starting point to learning about what Catholics believe. If you're looking for deeper answers, check out resources I've provided.

Peace be with you,

Danielle

Danielle Schaaf

The Nicene Creed

I believe in one God,
the Father almighty,
maker of heaven and earth,
of all things visible and invisible.

I believe in one Lord Jesus Christ,
the Only Begotten Son of God,
born of the Father before all ages.
God from God, Light from Light,
true God from true God,
begotten, not made, consubstantial with the Father;
through him all things were made.
For us men and for our salvation
he came down from heaven,

and by the Holy Spirit was incarnate of the Virgin Mary,
and became man.

For our sake he was crucified under Pontius Pilate,
he suffered death and was buried,
and rose again on the third day
in accordance with the Scriptures.
He ascended into heaven
and is seated at the right hand of the Father.
He will come again in glory
to judge the living and the dead
and his kingdom will have no end.

I believe in the Holy Spirit, the Lord, the giver of life,
who proceeds from the Father and the Son,

112

Holy Bones, Limbo, and Jesus in My Cheetos

who with the Father and the Son is adored and glorified,
who has spoken through the prophets.

I believe in one, holy, catholic and apostolic Church.
I confess one Baptism for the forgiveness of sins
and I look forward to the resurrection of the dead
and the life of the world to come. Amen.

Danielle Schaaf

Resources

Catechism of the Catholic Church

Catholic Online: www.catholic.org

United States Conference of Catholic Bishops (parish locator): www.usccb.org

Catholics Returning Home: www.catholicsreturninghome.org

Catholic Home Study: www.catholichomestudy.org

Divine Litany of Acknowledgments

Vicki Quade,
For helping restart my creative cogs when they ground to a halt, and for nailing the subtitle,
I gratefully appreciate and acknowledge you.

Gayle Hogwood,
For reading the manuscript and making sure I didn't stray too far off the Catholic path,
I gratefully appreciate and acknowledge you.

Alex Schaaf,
For reviewing sports references and fine-tuning the comparison of Church hierarchy to Major League Baseball,
I gratefully appreciate and acknowledge you.

Kristen Schaaf,
For putting up with my son's never-ending obsession with sports, which he put to good use reviewing my manuscript,
I gratefully appreciate and acknowledge you.

Hannah and Andrew Schaaf,
For alerting me to details in Peyton Manning's life, which reinforced my decision to send him on the road to sainthood,
I gratefully appreciate and acknowledge you.

Cat Schaaf,
For sharing with me intricacies of door stacking and other slices of sorority life,
I gratefully appreciate and acknowledge you.

Mark Schaaf,
For enlightening me with your non-Catholic perspective, especially about who gets left behind during the rapture,
I gratefully appreciate and acknowledge you.

Carrie Kabak,
For designing my stunning and totally spot-on book cover,
I gratefully appreciate and acknowledge you.

Lisa Cerasoli,
For sharing your keen eye, sharp editing skills, and sense of humor,
I gratefully appreciate and acknowledge you.

Stacey Fitzpatrick,
For providing eagle-eye proofreading and witty commentary,
I gratefully appreciate and acknowledge you.

Lilia Fabry,
For formatting my manuscript and answering my non-stop questions,
I gratefully appreciate and acknowledge you.

Sally Cooper and Adela Holda,
For supporting me with kind words, laughter, and wine,
I gratefully appreciate and acknowledge you.

Kristina Riggle, Maggie Dana, Eliza Graham, Jill Morrow, Becky Motew, Marina Richards, Carrie Kabak
For cheering me on, offering advice, and showering me with inspiration,
I gratefully appreciate and acknowledge you.

St. Luke Catholic School Sisters of Mercy,
For creating the framework of this book so many years ago,
I gratefully appreciate and acknowledge you.

About the Author

Danielle Schaaf is coauthor of Don't Chew Jesus! A Collection of Memorable Nun Stories. She is the creator of Haute Flash Contessa humor columns and comedy shows. After all these years, she's still Catholic and even taught Catholic religious education to children for ten years. To her knowledge, none were scarred. Married, and the mother of three children, Danielle resides in Houston.

60227275R00073

Made in the USA
San Bernardino, CA
10 December 2017